ISBN: 978-0-9657828-3-8

Book Cover Design and Formating by Elev8 Designs Co. | www.elev8designs.co

TESTIMONIALS

"The Hilliers crushed it! All I can say is, "Wow, this book is unreal!" If you are ready to stop participating and start DOMINATING, read this book five times, master the skills, and do the drills. If you do, you will never be the same. It's that simple. So quit settling for average, and start pushing the sled!"

-Brian Cain | Creator of Mental Performance Mastery Certification

"Push the Sled is a great book to read. It's full of wisdom, it's entertaining, and I highly recommend it. Go out and get it!"

- Chris Voss | Author of the best selling book, Never Split the Difference

"Push the Sled is an invigorating tale that vividly captures the essence of competitive spirit and the power of personal growth. DJ Hillier masterfully navigates the reader through the highs and lows of high school athletics, infusing each page with the intensity and heart that defines the journey of an athlete. But this book is not just a story about sports; it's a guide on leadership, perseverance, and the relentless pursuit of excellence. Hillier's narrative resonates with anyone who has ever faced the daunting yet exhilarating challenge of pushing beyond their limits to achieve the extraordinary."

-Marshall Goldsmith | #1 Executive Coach and New York Times Best Selling Author of What Got You Here Won't Get You There

"Push the Sled is packed with useful lessons and practical strategies on how to be the best version of yourself in sport and in life."

-Justin Su'a | Process and Development Advisor to Professional Sports Organizations in the NFL, NHL, and MLB

"This book is a MUST READ for athletes looking to elevate their mental game and attack the gap between where they are and where they want to be!"

-Sean Casey | 3x MLB All-Star

"Push the Sled redefines the path to success, with compelling stories and practical advice that fuel personal growth. This book will inspire you to push beyond your comfort zone and become a better version of yourself. A must-read for anyone ready to elevate their game."

-Lauren Johnson | Advisor, Coach, Speaker, and former Mental Performance Coach for the New York Yankees

"Phenomenal! A huge part of sports and life is what happens "in between your ears." Push the Sled delivers solid ideas in a fun, story format that can be applied immediately. As a former NBA player and current Hall of Fame motivational speaker, I can attest to the idea that Separation through Preparation will be the difference between being average or being exceptional. I only wish I could have read this book in high school!"

-Walter Bond | Former NBA player, Author of the book Swim, Hall of Fame motivational speaker

"Push The Sled" is a timeless guide to mastering the art of achieving greatness in every aspect of life. Drawing from the concepts of sports psychology, authors DJ and Craig Hiller take readers on a journey of self-discovery and personal growth. Through simple and captivating storytelling, this book offers invaluable lessons on the power of dedication, self awareness, and resilience. Whether you're striving for success in your career, athletics, or personal endeavors, "Push The Sled" provides the tools and inspiration to overcome obstacles, stay focused on your goals, and ultimately, live a fulfilling and purpose-driven life.

-Ben Bergeron | CrossFit Games Coach, Affiliate Owner, Author of Chasing Excellence

Push the Sled is a game changer! As a bowling coach who has given over 25,000 lessons from entry level to top pros, I know developing a strong mental game is vital for success. The strategies on dealing with pressure were especially meaningful. In bowling, if you need three strikes in the 10th frame to win the match, without unshakable confidence and a strong mental game–you're history. This is a must read for handling clutch moments!

-Mark Baker | Former Professional Bowler, Team USA bowling coach, Author of the book Game Changer .

PUSH THE SLED

DEDICATION

To Kelly, Ashley, Abby, Holly and Kinsley. We love you very much.

SPECIAL THANKS

Thanks to super star mental performance coach Brian Cain. The time we shared in Arizona outlining and collaborating on the book was magical. Your dedication to helping people in all walks develop a winning mindset is phenomenal. Push the Sled would not have happened without your energy and expertise!

Thanks to our fabulous editor Diane Brown, our amazing graphic designer Sarah Dissegna, and our famous photographer Joe Dickie. Josh Bergan and Leah Hamilton were awesome models for the photos. Every one of you knocked it out of the park!

TABLE OF CONTENTS

TABLE OF CONTENTS

TABLE OF CONTENTS

PREFACE
INTRODUCTION

"Jackson, You're in!"

The stadium was silent. I grabbed my helmet and walked over to Coach Allen, my heart beating through my chest.

Coach put his hands on my shoulder pads and said, "Jackson, you're a heck of an athlete and a great competitor. The injury out there looks pretty severe.

We're counting on you to step in, be the quarterback and the leader for this team. We're down 14-0 with 8:17 left. We can still win this thing!"

My eyes were wide. At first, I thought it was a dream. I couldn't believe I was stepping into my first varsity game in the fourth quarter against our cross-town rival in a playoff game!

I ran out to the huddle to meet my teammates. By the looks on their faces, I could tell they had lost hope.

"We've got this, guys! This season isn't over."

The first play was a run play that went fourteen yards. The stadium went from radio silent to loud cheers, and we were getting into rhythm.

After a nine play drive, we finished with a touchdown from our all-conference tailback.

After the scoring drive, we jogged off to the sidelines, where I was met

1

by a bunch of teammates giving me high fives and words of encouragement.

Man, this is pretty fun! I thought.

Converting the extra point made it 14-7.

Our defense came up with a huge fourth down stop, and we got the ball back with 1:51 left in the game.

Coach called for our two-minute offense and reminded me that we didn't have any timeouts left.

One pass after another, I was zinging the ball to our receivers. After each catch, they stepped out of bounds immediately to stop the clock.

Is this really happening? Am I, the back-up quarterback, leading this team on a game winning drive? I couldn't believe it.

I spiked the ball on the ten yard line to stop the clock with four seconds left.

We had one play, and we needed to get into the end zone.

Coach called a roll out to the right side where I would find our receiver on a comeback route right at the pylon.

Sure enough, he was there, and I delivered the ball on a tightrope right between the numbers on his chest.

Touchdown! I pumped my fist in the air.

14-13. *Only down by 1. Let's go!*

I immediately looked over at Coach Allen on the sideline. He had two fingers in the air signifying he wanted to go for two and get the win.

I nodded back at him and smiled. We had momentum on our side and the crowd was going bananas.

This was it. One play to determine if the season was over or if we advanced to the state tournament.

As we walked up to the line of scrimmage, the stadium erupted.

"DOWN... SET... HUT!" I yelled at the top of my lungs.

2

I went into my three-step drop, looked right, saw our receiver open, and let the ball float into the corner of the endzone.

Interception.

I fell to one knee in total disbelief.

CHAPTER 1
THE FINAL SCORE

14-13. Those numbers were the background on my cell phone lock screen.

It was a play that I had replayed in my mind so many times since it had happened that I'd lost count.

Our receiver was wide open, but I underthrew the ball right to the other team for an interception. The sound of our rival's band fight song still echoes in my mind. Seeing their fans rush OUR field was a memory I couldn't erase.

Man, did I hear it.

"Jackson, you suck!"

"The pressure got ya number 5?"

"Better grab some water before you choke again."

"Hit the road, toad!" This was a jab on our dumb mascot.

Those were the nicer comments. The stuff on social media was brutal. I wanted to stop looking at it, but I was obsessed with what others thought.

I was one play away from being the hero and ended up being the goat. Not "The Greatest of All Time" but the older version of the goat, the person who makes the big mistake that costs his team the game. Instead of being a hero, I felt like a zero.

Our baseball coach once showed us a video clip of some guy named Bill Buckner who lost focus in a World Series game and let an easy grounder roll right between his legs. I could already see myself becoming the Bill Buckner of Pine Lake High School.

Coach Allen had prepared us to run that specific play on a two-point conversion should the situation present itself.

I felt prepared. I just didn't execute.

14-13 was my motivation.

14-13 was what drove me.

Unlike most of the kids, I couldn't wait for summer training to start. But was I truly ready to be the full-time starter?

Despite the last play failure, my teammates had elected me as one of the captains after the season wrapped up. I was excited and nervous about this role. I was excited because it was an honor to be a captain. I was nervous because I wasn't the best player on the team.

At Pine Lake High School, a mid-size school in a suburb of Minneapolis, the teams all combined for a summer conditioning program so that we could pool our coaches and equipment resources.

I liked training with other athletes and friends on various teams.

My twin sister, on the other hand, hated it.

Scan the QR Code to watch the
Bill Buckner Clip

CHAPTER 2

OLIVIA

Ever since we got involved in youth sports, she was the twin who was considered the premier athlete in the family. Gifted, explosive, and talented.

Just not all that hardworking in school or sports.

How she had a 3.8 GPA was beyond me. Her phone never stopped dinging with notifications from friends. To top it off, there was no shortage of social interest for her. Last year, she had to decide between three *promposals*.

Olivia participated in individual and team-based sports. She was the number two player on her tennis team in the fall but could have been number one.

She was in gymnastics in the winter and ran track in the spring. She despised the summer strength and conditioning program. I always had to drag her with me. She always seemed to find an excuse or blame others for her apparent lack of results for what we all thought she could accomplish.

When my parents were still together, they always told us that if they could combine my drive with Olivia's talent, they would have an Olympian in the family.

That summer, we were to get a new strength coach at Pine Lake. I hoped that she might be able to bring some more energy and life to our summer training. Maybe she could get through to Olivia about her work ethic.

CHAPTER 3
THE NEW HIRE

For the past ten years, Coach Johnson had run the summer strength and conditioning program.

Coach Johnson was chill. He was a big ol' former college offensive lineman who loved to squat, bench, and deadlift. Summer training ONLY revolved around those three lifts combined with a one-mile run. Oliva was not a fan. Much to her satisfaction, he was not going to be with us anymore, as he had taken a new coaching job at another school.

Coach Allen was our athletic director and head football coach. He assured us that the new coach he hired was going to not only push us to be the best version of ourselves physically but also mentally. Rumor was the new strength coach was fresh out of training at the Olympic Training Center in Colorado. Coach Allen told a few of us this new hire could help all athletes improve inside and outside our sport.

After the final bell of the year rang, kids ran out the doors to start their summer vacation. I headed to the auditorium with 149 others for Coach Allen's year ending/year beginning meeting. He would be kicking off the summer strength and conditioning program.

We entered the auditorium to a highlight video from the previous year. This was new. *Too bad I didn't complete the pass. Then I would have been in it.*

CHAPTER 4

THE GREATEST GIFT YOU CAN GIVE

Coach Allen then grabbed the mic and, in his head football coach voice, said, "Give me two claps."

"Let's try that again. TWO CLAPS!" Coach Allen said.

This time we were much louder.

"That's better. Remember, if you're juiceful, you're useful, and if you're juiceless, you're useless. We need to bring the juice here to this meeting. Last year finished a few moments ago. It's history. Right now, this year is the only one that any of us can do anything about." I could feel the intensity in the room start to pick up.

"Pine Lake, the greatest gift that you can give to yourself, your team, and your school is your presence. **Your presence is the greatest gift you can give.** I thank you for being here, and I am beyond excited for your upcoming seven-week summer training that will lead us into the fall. Seniors, please stand up!

"My twenty years as a coach and ten years as an athletic director has taught me that ninety percent of the time, the senior class creates the spirit, morale, and culture in school and extra curriculars. Seniors, this may sound silly, but you are officially no longer juniors. We will be looking to you to lead us to and through an amazing year," said Coach Allen.

I couldn't believe that the time had come. I was now a senior. I only played in a few drives because I was a backup to one of the best athletes in school history. He had been our starting quarterback and was headed to the University of Minnesota on a full scholarship. It was now my time to take on a bigger role.

I was looking forward to helping my team "out-compete the competition," as Coach Allen would say.

As I looked around the room at the other seniors who were standing up, including my twin, Olivia, I knew that this summer was going to be critical.

We hadn't always had the best turnout for summer conditioning. I wasn't sure why, maybe it was that kids had summer jobs. Maybe it was because it was in the morning. Maybe it was because people didn't like the repetitive heavy lifting that Coach Johnson programmed. We often talked about going the extra mile, but the only mile most of us ran was the one after we lifted. In general, Pine Lake athletes usually settled for slightly over average effort. I wasn't sure what the reason was, but I hoped my final summer would be different.

If we were going to make it to State this year, we had a lot of work in front of us.

CHAPTER 5
THE TIME IS N:OW

"The time is now..." Coach Allen said as he clicked to the next slide.

"And the place is here."

"Let's do this loud and proud. The time is..." he cupped his ear.

"NOW!" we shouted back.

Then he asked, "The place is where?"

"HERE!" we thundered.

"Now, everyone on your feet. Let me introduce you to the newest member of our family. Please put your hands together for our new strength coach and physical education teacher, Coach Jessica Whitlock," Coach Allen said enthusiastically. We all clapped as a tall woman wearing an UNRL Team USA shirt walked forward from the back of the stage. She stood next to Coach Allen at the podium. Her blonde hair was in a ponytail, and it was easy to see she was in excellent shape. She could probably out-lift and out-sprint eighty percent of us.

Coach Allen continued, "She was a sprinter at the University of Minnesota and then went on to compete for a spot on the Team USA Olympic bobsled team. She trained with intensity and earned a spot as an alternate, prepared to take any of the four positions on the team. Although she didn't get the chance to compete in the Games, her preparation and perseverance were amazing. One more round of applause for Coach Whitlock!"

She stepped up to the mic. "Thank you. Please take your seats. As Coach Allen said, I haven't competed in an Olympic event. But I want to add one word to that sentence. I haven't competed in an official Olympic event yet," she said with a confident smile. "Not yet."

Something in the way she carried herself gave me the impression that she was the real deal.

"I want to try something. When I say CHECK IN, I want all of you to respond with ALL IN," she said.

"CHECK IN!"

"ALL IN!" we called back.

"I'm not a gambler whatsoever. And even though I don't understand poker much, I love watching it on TV. My favorite part is the ALL IN moment. There is a pivotal point when a player has taken everything into consideration. They know the situation, the strength of their cards, the way their opponent plays, and they make a conscious decision to push all their chips to the center of the table. Boldly saying ALL IN.

"In that moment, they totally believe one of two things. One, they believe they have the best hand and if their opponent calls, they will win. Or two, they believe their opponent doesn't have enough faith in their hand, so they will quit and fold. In poker, does the best hand always win? No. The person who plays their hand the best wins. Sometimes having the conviction to go ALL IN even with weak cards scares off a player who has a better hand.

In sports, does the best team or individual always win? No, the team or individual who plays the best usually does.

You don't win in poker, sports, or life without having the courage to push all your chips to the middle. ALL IN is about confidence, courage and believing.

So, this summer, when any of the coaches say CHECK IN, we want to hear ALL IN! back from you. It must be said with conviction, courage, and confidence that you are committed to putting all your chips, or in this case all your energy, effort, and focus into this program."

The auditorium was silent. She had everyone's attention.

"Pine Lake, I am thrilled to be your new strength coach. As Coach Allen said, 'The time is now, and the place is here.' I am here to help you maximize your potential. Look, there's no substitute for strength and conditioning and no excuse for a lack of it. It's one aspect of athletic performance, over which you have complete control.

"This summer, we will dominate the controllables. This summer, we will get you into the best shape of your life. That requires you to also get into the best mental shape of your life.

"Here's what your summer schedule looks like. Please take out your phones and scan this QR code on the screen.

"We will meet right here every Monday for Mental Performance Mondays. I can promise you that the sixty to ninety minutes we invest each week on our minds will be as impactful, if not more so, than what we do on the field. The mental and physical work we do will test and transform you."

13

CHAPTER 6
GET TO VERSUS HAVE TO

As I took out my phone, I was impressed with Coach Whitlock's energy, passion, and athletic background. I was just unsure about these Mental Performance Mondays.

As we pulled up the summer schedule on our phones, there were a few gasps.

"This summer, we get to be here Monday through Thursday mornings, from 6:00 to 8:00," said coach Whitlock.

"You said we get to be here from 6:00 to 8:00 in the morning. Don't you mean we have to be here from 6:00 to 8:00?" said a student who wasn't called on by the new coach.

"Good question. What's your name?"

"David Kinger. Everyone just calls me Kinger," said the often cocky two-time all-conference running back who sat behind me.

"I guess it depends on your perspective. If you see it like we get to be here, it becomes a privilege. I've visited countries around the world where kids would love the opportunity to be here at 6:00 and be a part of the program you are about to experience. If you look at it as we have to be here, it becomes a chore. It's your choice. None of the coaches will be calling you or your guardians if you skip out. I sleep the same way whether you're here or not. If you don't see the value in what we're doing, sleep in. At the end of the day, it's your call, Kinger."

She cleared her throat, "So, as I was saying, the summer will be divided into two parts. We start this coming Monday and go for three weeks. The week of July 4th we will take off.

"We will pick it back up the second week of July and go through the first week of August. For the fall athletes, you then have a week break before your season's kickoff."

Coach Whitlock clicked to the next slide. "Wednesday will be known as Winning Edge Wednesday. A guest speaker will join us for each of these.

"Going back to the earlier question. We get to work out at 6:00 a.m. this year to accommodate those of you who have a summer job. We will work hard this summer because work wins!

"WORK WHAT?" Whitlock asked the group as she rolled her hands out.

"WINS!" we all replied.

"That's right. Work wins, period!

"We will be working harder and smarter by getting after it when the sun is coming up twenty-eight times this summer. We will sweat before screens. TikTok and texting can wait until eight. I doubt our opponents will be up as early as we are.

"Let's be clear, elite performance happens in your mind first. It's a decision, and your decisions determine your destiny. Elite performers are willing to do what others are not willing to do, even when they don't feel like it.

"I'm not just talking about winning more games. I'm talking about winning beyond the scoreboard."

Coach Whitlock was bringing the juice. I wasn't sure what Olivia or my teammates thought of her vibe, but I loved it.

"The man who taught me things like playing to a standard, not the scoreboard, the importance of the mental game and how to train physically to create your competitive advantage is my father, Robert Towns. Because of his passion, intensity, and loyalty to his teammates, his fellow Olympians affectionally nicknamed him Bobby Bobsled."

I could hear laughter behind me, so I glanced back.

"Bobby Bobsled...lame...real original," snickered Kinger. He thought of himself as the King of Comebacks. While some of his comebacks were funny, most of them were not. Plus, his timing was usually terrible.

CHAPTER 7
BOBBY BOBSLED

Robert Towns, a.k.a. Bobby Bobsled, walked out from the back of the stage just as Coach Whitlock had. My guess was that he was in his late sixties or early seventies, but he looked to still be in phenomenal shape. He rocked a full head of snow-white hair and a short beard that covered his strong jaw line. For a guy his age, his forearms were massive. He looked like he could still put up a competitive 40 time.

"My dad is here for the summer helping my husband and me with a fixer-upper house we bought down the street. He's not only the handiest person I know, but he is also the best coach I know," Coach Whitlock said with a big smile. "He was a two-time member of the Team USA bobsled team in the 1980s and to this day holds the United States record for fastest sled push to start a race. He will be here for the summer coaching with me, along with the rest of our staff."

"Together, we created your summer strength and conditioning program. We are excited to serve you and to help all of you attack the gap from where you are to where you want to be. All we ask from you is to give us all you got."

Coach Whitlock went back to the slide and repeated, "The time is now, the place is here. Enjoy your weekend. We will see you here Monday morning at precisely 6:00 for day one of the Separation Through Preparation program. Remember, mentally strong athletes show up prepared and on time. This summer, instead of counting the days, let's make the days count."

CHAPTER 8
A MIXED REACTION

As we all walked out of the auditorium that afternoon, there were mixed reactions. Some of the athletes, including me, were fired up to have Coach Whitlock and Bobby with us. She and her dad seemed to know what they were doing. At least they looked the part and had the resumes to prove it.

Others, including Olivia, were skeptical.

She complained, "I thought Coach Johnson's training sucked. Who is this boomer Bobby Bobsled? What does bobsledding have to do with tennis, gymnastics, or track? Why can't we ever get someone here who knows what they're doing? Mental Performance Mondays, you can't 'mentally condition.' You either have it or you don't. Winning Edge Wednesdays with some boring speaker. What a joke. Can't believe this trash."

I was used to my twin sister and her negative reaction to anything new. If it wasn't her idea, she wasn't buying into it. That was Olivia. Unfortunately, it was also the attitude of some of my teammates. The feedback and social posts that day were not exactly positive for Coach Whitlock and Bobby Bobsled.

It was surprising to see how quick people were to judge the new coaches after just one meeting.

It wasn't long after the meeting that the conversation on social shifted from the new coaches to that night's party.

18

CHAPTER 9
THE SPOT

The first weekend of the summer started with what we called "Bash at the Beach." We met at a hidden reserve area on the far side of the lake where homes weren't allowed to be built. Nobody went there other than high school kids. The first beach bash of the summer was usually pretty lit.

I wasn't a big party guy, but I liked to hang out with my teammates. It was a cool place to chill, and there was usually a huge campfire where we hung out before the park ranger would come by around midnight and send everyone home.

On my way to the beach, I drove by the high school and saw that the stadium lights were on. I drove into the parking lot to see what was going on, parked in the first row, and walked to the fence. No one was in sight. Confused, I walked onto the field and found myself standing on "the spot."

There I was again, at the two-and-a-half-yard line on the right side of the field, facing the scoreboard. Although the scoreboard was off, I could still see 14-13.

CHAPTER 10
PROVE IT

"What are you doing our here so late son?" a voice asked behind me.

I jumped a little and turned around. My fear calmed when I recognized it was Bobby Bobsled. He was wearing a gray t-shirt with the Team USA logo on it. It was covered in sweat and the muscles in his chest and arms were popping. He was fillin' the sleeves.

"Everything alright?" asked Bobby.

"Yeah, I was driving by and wondered why the lights were on," I replied.

"Well, I was just making sure all the equipment was ready for Monday. Robert Towns," he said, and we shook hands. His hands were strong, callused, and rough. This confirmed what I saw in the auditorium. He was a man who used his hands for work.

"My friends call me Bobby. My daughter is the new strength coach here at the high school, and she twisted my arm to help her with that fixer-upper she bought across the street," he pointed to the run-down house with siding in multiple colors and weeds over three feet tall.

"It's rough now, but wait till you see the plans we have for it. Anyway, then she twisted more and talked me into helping with the summer conditioning camp." Bobby smirked. "Truth is, she didn't need to twist much. I'd do anything for my daughter."

"I'm Jackson Pierce. Yeah, I know you. You're Bobby Bobsled. I liked what you guys were talking about at today's meeting."

"Thanks. We're in for an amazing summer. At least those who stick with it are. Sounds like that's been a problem here. Not finishing," Bobby said. "Hey, none of my business, but are you sure the only reason you're here is to see why the lights were on?"

"At first, yes. Then I was just replaying a stupid play from last year."

"Which play are you talking about?" asked Bobby.

"I threw an interception from right about here that not only cost us the game but it ended our season. It's a play that's on repeat in my head. I need to prove some people wrong this year."

"I actually watched that game. Coach Allen provided links to game film of each sport for Jess and me. We both wanted to see who we would be working with this summer. You played well for coming off the bench cold with no varsity experience. That's not easy."

"Thanks," I said with a smile. "I didn't have any time to think. They just yelled my name and sent me out there. I played well, just not well enough to win. I guess that's the real reason I'm here tonight."

"Well, there are a few ways to motivate yourself. One is what you're doing now, thinking about proving others wrong," Bobby said. "There is certainly power in that. Feels good to stick it in the doubters' faces. I still remember the look on the Russian's faces when we stuck it to them in the quarterfinals. It was satisfying. But only for a few minutes. See, that can be a problem, if you always need to prove someone wrong. As soon as you accomplish something, you need to find another hater!

"Jackson, since that game, have you spent more time thinking about the one play that didn't go your way or the nine other passes you completed for over a hundred yards and a touchdown I believe?" Bobby asked.

"Yeah, I know. But I can't stop thinking about how the game ended."

I took out my phone and showed Bobby the background on my screen. 14-13 in large numbers.

Bobby raised his eyebrows, "Let me tell you something. **A bad chapter doesn't define the book**. If you want to play well this fall, maybe it's time to add another form of motivation" Bobby said. "Do you find yourself constantly competing to prove other people wrong?"

"For sure," I answered.

"Have you ever considered competing to try and prove yourself right?"

"Not really."

Bobby replied, "It's a balancing act. See, if you only play to prove someone else wrong, you start playing angry and not enjoying the process. If you compete only to prove yourself right, sometimes you go too easy on yourself and don't push yourself to grind it out. The elite athletes can figure out when to use each approach. Sometimes they go back and forth several times a day! Balance is key, Jackson. You must have physical and mental balance in order to be an outstanding athlete.

"I get what you're saying, Bobby. I just can't get the image of the final score on that scoreboard out of my mind."

"As Olympic athletes, we learned it was better to review a performance than to relive it. That way, you digest the lesson, you give yourself a gift, and you let it go."

I had never thought of it that way before, so I just stared at Bobby Bobsled, taking it all in.

"What I've learned from being in sports for over fifty years is the highest forms of mental toughness are acceptance and forgiveness. Contrary to what most people believe, perfectionism is the lowest because it's just not attainable. Great athletes are resilient, not perfect.

"My friend Dr. Jim Afremow said it best: 'When it comes to a mistake or poor performance, the new mental game is how fast can you get over it instead of how long will you hang on to it?'"

CHAPTER 11
IT'S THE BOUNCE THAT COUNTS!

Bobby took out a little red Superball from his pocket. "I've been carrying one of these around since 1980." He threw it on the track so hard that it bounced way above our heads. "Jackson, it's the bounce that counts."

Bobsled Bobby caught the ball on its descent and handed it to me. "Keep it, kid. I have a drawer full."

"Thanks, Coach." As I put the Superball in my pocket, I grabbed my phone. "Let me get this in my notes app before I forget it."

"You've given me a lot to think about," I said, thankfully.

"Good," said Bobby. **"Your thoughts determine what you want. Your actions determine what you get.** Thinking is a small part of the mental game. The bigger part is the action you take."

"Hey, if you're going to go by 'Action Jackson,' we need you to take more action this summer."

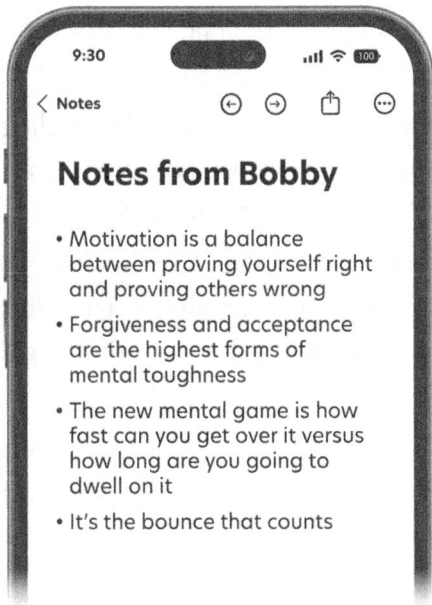

9:30   .ııl 🛜 100

< Notes   ← → ⬆ ⋯

Notes from Bobby

- Motivation is a balance between proving yourself right and proving others wrong
- Forgiveness and acceptance are the highest forms of mental toughness
- The new mental game is how fast can you get over it versus how long are you going to dwell on it
- It's the bounce that counts

CHAPTER 12
ACTION CHANGES EVERYTHING

"How did you know they called me 'Action Jackson'?" I asked with a laugh.

"Good question. As I said, Jess and I did our homework on the group. Coach Allen did a good job filling us in on the key leaders in the summer program. That's how I knew you, son.

As an athlete, you're always being watched. People know who you are, so how you carry yourself matters. Whether it's school, eating at a restaurant with your buddies, or walking around Pine Lake, a lot of people know who you are, so be aware of that.

Thinking is a part of becoming better. You can excel by understanding the combination of thinking and doing. It's worth repeating—your thoughts determine what you want. Your actions determine what you get."

What Bobby said was making a lot of sense. When Coach Whitlock mentioned Mental Performance Mondays, it sounded cool, but I didn't really know what she meant. As I listened to Bobby, I was starting to get the picture.

Bobby continued, "Results come to those who Understand that **action changes everything.** I call it ACE! If you are going to be the ace of the baseball pitching staff next spring or the ace of the offense as quarterback or the ace of this summer's Separation Through Preparation program, you need to focus on how you act. I'd encourage you to act on reviewing the fourteen plays you executed well in that final game instead of reliving one you'd like to have back."

"Thanks again, Bobby. You've given me a lot to think about and a lot to take action on," I said. "I'm excited to get to work with you."

With that, we shook hands again, and I started walking toward my car to head to the beach. Little did I know that my brief interaction with Bobby was just the tip of the iceberg when it came to the depth of knowledge that he and Coach Whitlock had in store for us that summer.

I was really hoping that Bobby and Coach Whitlock would help me get over the pass that got away. I knew I needed to let that go to be a better athlete and leader. It just seemed impossible.

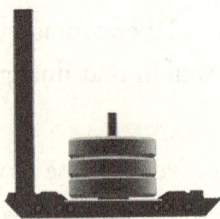

CHAPTER 13
THE BEACH

When I finally got to the beach, there were a ton of kids there. Most were on their phones texting and snapping people who were already there. My mom always made fun of me for this, but it was what we did.

I joined Olivia and a group of our friends by the fire pit.

"What's up, Action?" asked Kinger with a cocky tone.

"Nothin', Kinger. Just chillin'," I said.

"Where you been, man? Not like you to be late, unless it's throwing an out route in the end zone," he said sarcastically. This brought a cheap laugh as people looked up from their phones. Even my sister laughed.

Kinger was a physically talented athlete who talked a big game but didn't feel he had to work that hard given his level of talent. He was clearly the best player on the team but was openly frustrated that I had been chosen as a captain. He had been a two-year starter, while I hadn't started a game yet. Coach Allen told me privately I was voted captain because I was the best player for the team.

"Good one, bro," I said with a laugh on the outside but with my blood still boiling. "I stopped by the school and actually ran into Bobby Bobsled."

CHAPTER 14
THE BASH

"Those two strength coaches were bobsledders. What are bobsledders going to teach me about being a better football player? Kinger said selfishly. "It's going to be another wasted summer. Speaking of wasted, maybe we should just get wasted instead!" This time, no one laughed at the "King of Comebacks."

For the next hour it was a bash, where people were celebrating the end of school while bashing the new coaches, schedule, and overall program. This was a classic "Bash at the Beach." I started to wonder why I even came to these things.

Pine Lake was known for talented teams and talented athletes, like Kinger. But we also had a reputation for underperforming in the playoffs.

We were a school where so many students thought it was cool to be sarcastic, yet our hallways had multiple banners that read "It's Cool to Be Kind."

Listening to all the trash talk, I felt discouraged that the other kids didn't seem as excited about our new program as I was. Bobby and Coach Whitlock had their work cut out for them.

CHAPTER 15
THE COACHES' MEETING

Monday was day one of the new program. I wanted to be one of the first ones there, so I arrived at 5:35 a.m. Nine weeks from today would be the first official day of practice for all fall sports.

Although the auditorium doors were locked, I could hear Coach Whitlock telling the other coaches how the day was going to go. I had no idea that our coaches prepared like this. In the past, it felt like Coach Johnson just winged it.

But she was fired up. "Remember, energy is our edge, and our energy is contagious, so let's just be sure it's worth catching. **Coaches, if you want your team to be energized, then you need to be energized.** We want these two hours each morning to be the highlight of their entire day so they can't wait to come back tomorrow. If it doesn't challenge them, it won't change them."

Coach Whitlock was organized, spoke clearly and had tons of energy.

Loud music blared as the doors opened at 5:50. The right and left sides of the auditorium were taped off. The only place to sit was in the center section. I found myself sitting in the front row. That was new for me.

It was almost 6:00, and the center seats were nearly filled up. A few athletes, led by Kinger, tried to hop over the tape and sit in the side sections. This was classic Kinger. Coaches immediately asked them to sit in the center.

This summer was already on a different level than last year.

CHAPTER 16
ALL IN

At 6:00 a.m. sharp, Coach Whitlock started the meeting with a loud "CHECK IN!"

"ALL IN!" we replied.

"Everyone who can stand, please get on your feet. Please stand tall with shoulders back. Stand proud to be a Pine Lake athlete," she commanded.

As we all stood up in unison, I could feel the reluctancy in the room.

"When one of your coaches asks you to check in, you repeat back, 'ALL IN.' Last week, I talked about what this meant for me. Now, what's that mean to you? I want you to think about that for a second." She paused. "Now, pair up and talk to the person next to you about what it means to be 'All In.'"

Coach Whitlock used her iPad to write our responses and project them on the screen.

This was new for us. We were used to just being told what to do instead of being asked what we thought. In the past, we just lifted weights.

She circled *be present* on her iPad. "A major piece of being 'all in' means you are where your feet are. At any given moment, you could have one foot in the past, dwelling on what has already happened, and one foot in the future, anxious about what's coming up next. The best athletes and competitors have both feet firmly planted in the present, right here, right

29

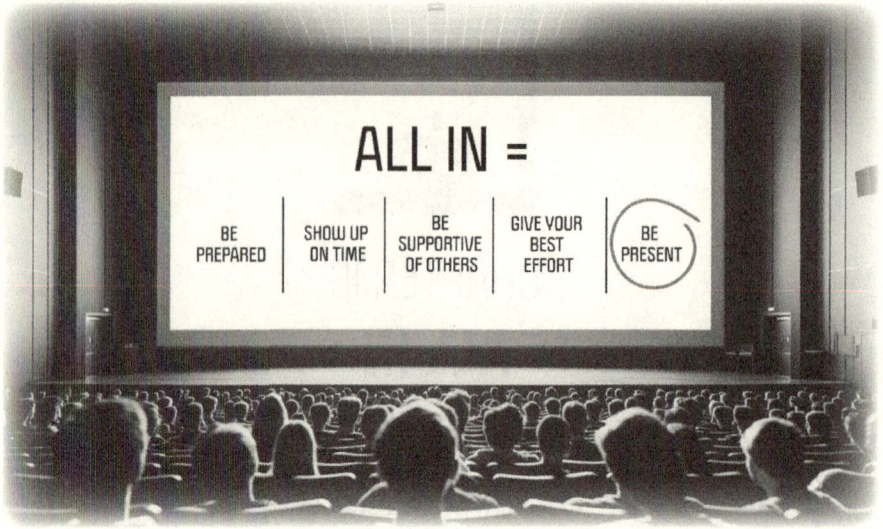

now," she explained. "To be 'all in' means you are all in this moment. You are fully focused right here, right now. Anxiety often shows up when you focus too much on a future you can't control. Depression comes from focusing on a past you can't go back and change, a past that you have not yet accepted or forgiven yourself for. That's called history. Optimal performance, our goal, comes from being fully focused and 'all in' this moment.

"Now, you are all in this room at 6:00 on the first Monday of your summer. The question is, can you be into being in this room? **There's a huge difference between being in and being into.** If you are going to maximize your summer workouts, you need to be into what we're doing, not just in. What's it look like to be into versus just in?" Coach Whitlock asked.

We were asked to form groups of four and discuss the question.

CHAPTER 17
IN VERSUS INTO

Coach Whitlock then called on various athletes to share what they thought was the difference between in and into.

"*In* is just being in the room. *Into* is participating and taking notes."

"*In* is just showing up. *Into* is giving strong effort during meetings and workouts."

"*In* is just focusing on you. *Into* is focusing on your teammates in addition to yourself."

"All good answers. We have three themes that will help us get *into* this summer. The first theme is the name of the summer program, 'Separation Through Preparation.' The second theme is 'Little by little, a little becomes a lot,' because our goal is to get one percent better every day.

"We will get to the third theme in a few minutes. You have four shirts, two green and two black. Monday and Wednesday, we wear green. Tuesday and Thursday, we wear black.

"You will also get a white wristband with the imprinted letters STP and LBL. The STP stands for Separation Through Preparation, LBL stands for a Little Becomes a Lot."

With that, Coach Whitlock gave us ten minutes to grab our gear, training manuals, and change into our new shirts. We hustled back and continued with Mental Performance Monday.

CHAPTER 18
THE PLAN

"You might be wondering why we're kicking off each week focusing on mental performance? Let's brainstorm. What percent of your sport is mental? Think about it and go to page three in your binder and jot down your response."

After a minute, she had us talk to the other athletes near us.

"What did you come up with?" she asked.

"I'm a golfer, it's ninety percent mental," one athlete said.

"You mean ninety percent of golfers are mental," I heard the king of comebacks whisper a row behind me. A few laughs, but not many.

"I'm in cross country. I'd say eighty percent mental," another said.

"In lacrosse, it's probably fifty percent," another added.

"Thank you all for sharing. Based on your responses, it's clear that a large piece of performance in sports is mental. Here's the question. Are you investing as much time on the mental game as the percentage you wrote down?"

Almost every head shook sideways for a nonverbal no. Now she was starting to get some kids' attention.

"I was the same way until I went to the Olympic Training Center. We did a lot more mindset and mental performance training than we did in college," Coach Whitlock said. "Knowing what I know now, I wish that I had learned more about the mental game earlier in my career. I believe one hundred percent that it would have made a major difference for me.

Whitlock clicked to the next slide.

"Prior to being a part of team USA, I often bought into some of the myths of the mental game."

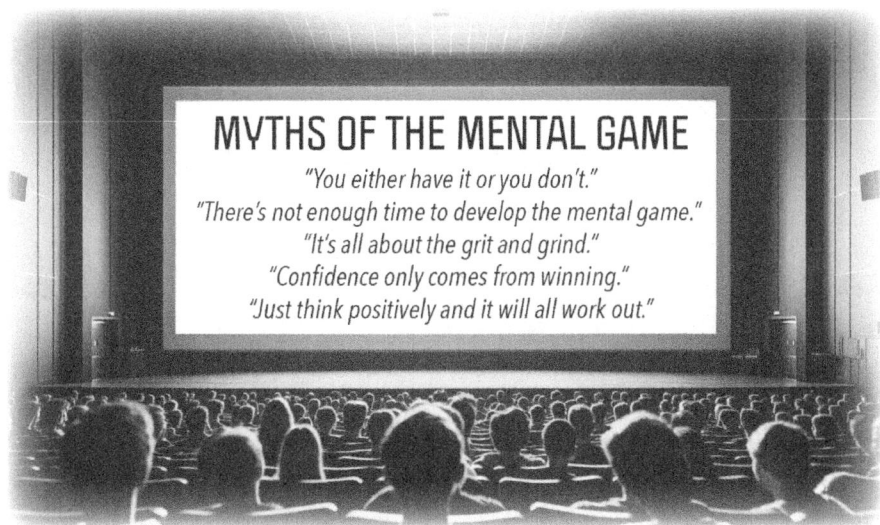

MYTHS OF THE MENTAL GAME

"You either have it or you don't."
"There's not enough time to develop the mental game."
"It's all about the grit and grind."
"Confidence only comes from winning."
"Just think positively and it will all work out."

"I'm very excited about having my dad here to help dismiss these myths by teaching drills to develop The 7 Tactical Skills of Mental Performance.

"These are the same seven skills that helped me make the Olympic team, and they are going to help you **attack the gap from where you are to where you want to be.** But you must do the work, because work wins. Work what?"

"WINS!" we all echoed back.

Bobby Bobsled walked onto the stage. "That's right, work wins. And if you want to win you need to clear the clutter in your mind and compete in the present moment.

"Competing in the present gives you the best chance for success.

The best chance to play your best when it means the most, and it means the most today. Today is the biggest day in the history of your life. Why? Because it's today. And today is the only day you are guaranteed.

CHAPTER 19
THE 7 TACTICAL SKILLS

"Go to page four in your training manual titled 'The 7 Tactical Skills of Optimal Mental Performance'," Bobby said.

"Tactical is a word you may not hear often, so I'll break it down for you. The definition of tactical is, **carefully planned actions, strategies, and maneuvers to gain a specific outcome.** For example, living in Minnesota, when driving through a snowstorm, we don't just cross our fingers and hope for the best. We want to have a tactical plan to get us to our destination safely. We can use the term tactical in what we are doing here this summer. For us, it's about taking our large goal of optimal mental and physical performance and breaking it down into manageable action steps to achieve our desired outcome.

We will explore these tactical skills each Mental Performance Monday. Our guest speakers will also expand on them during Winning Edge Wednesday."

"The best part about learning and building these skills is that they can be used now and for the rest of your life.

"We want this summer to be transformational, not transactional. Transformational is succeeding long term. Transactional is just exchanging your time for a workout. This manual will be a resource in your development as a person, student, and as an athlete.

"This could be a great summer of growth both physically and mentally for you. Champions are made in the off season. While most high school athletes are looking to bash at the beach, we will be pushing the sled and getting after it."

There was a hush over the auditorium. We all started looking at one another, wondering, How does he know about bash at the beach?

Suddenly, the auditorium curtain went up and our ten assistant coaches each pushed a sled to center stage.

These weren't bobsleds like Coach Bobby or Whitlock used on an ice track. These were brand new to our school. I'd seen similar sleds used in workouts online but never used one myself. They looked cool but kind of intimidating at the same time.

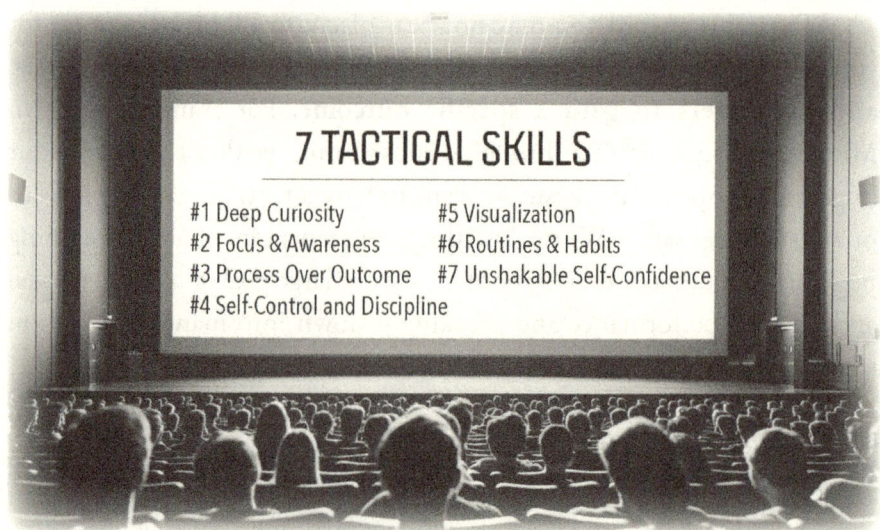

7 TACTICAL SKILLS

#1 Deep Curiosity   #5 Visualization
#2 Focus & Awareness   #6 Routines & Habits
#3 Process Over Outcome   #7 Unshakable Self-Confidence
#4 Self-Control and Discipline

CHAPTER 20
THE SLED

"The sled. Ahh... the lovely sled," Coach Whitlock said with a smile. "It has a special place in my heart and a special place in our training program. The sled is a versatile piece of equipment. It can be pushed forward or pulled backward. It can be loaded heavy for slow reps or light for enhancing speed and endurance. Sled workouts can be performed individually or as a team exercise. Plus, every one of us here is capable of pushing it. **My favorite part about the sled is that it tests your mind before it tests your body.**

"Obviously we're a bobsledding family, and now that we are a part of the Pine Lake family, we wanted to bring the sled to our daily workouts. The sleds can also be checked out from Coach Allen's office Monday through Thursday until 3:00. Sleds are a key part of our 'Champions Do More' workout series included in your manuals, for those of you wanting to do more so you can become more.

"As the Pine Lake coaching staff, we thought it would be fitting to get the new sleds customized for the school, so we asked the art department to paint our logo on them," Coach Whitlock said.

"At first glance, a Frog is probably not the most physically intimidating mascot out there."

We all nodded in agreement.

"However, the Ferocious Frog may be the best mascot in all of sports!"

CHAPTER 21
THE FROG

In an instant, the lights went out and a huge ferocious frog appeared on the screen. Bobby walked into the center of the spotlight.

"At one point, dinosaurs dominated life on earth. Through a long period of time and a series of events, the dinosaur, along with multiple other species of the wild, became extinct. Despite the odds and circumstances, some survived. One of the survivors included small amphibians called Anura. We commonly know them as frogs.

While there were only three families of Anura, they diversified rapidly. Right now, there are an estimated five thousand variants of frogs.

"So, how did the frog not only survive but thrive? One word... Adaptability. As amphibians, frogs are built to live a double life. If it isn't safe or suitable on land, they can hop in the water. Nothing to eat in the water? They head out on land to grab a bite.

"Frogs have adapted to environments on six continents, from low-lying deserts to the slopes of mountains at fifteen thousand feet. In the Australian outback, the water-holding frog can wait up to seven years for rain! Thanks to their cold blood, frogs can adapt their body temperature to their surroundings.

"Their legs provide extreme mobility, allowing them to leap up to twenty times their body length. That's equivalent to a hundred feet for you and me, essentially the length of this auditorium.

"The evolution of frogs proves that survival doesn't necessarily favor the strongest, like a dinosaur, but rather those lifeforms that are most adaptable, like a frog. The same is true for us as humans. We weren't the strongest species physically, but we had bigger brains. A bigger brain gave us the ability to think more deeply and ask better questions. This allowed us to adapt more effectively.

"The U.S. Navy SEALs are some of our nation's finest battle-tested warriors. They are often referred to as frogmen due to their adaptability and their ingenuity at finding the best way to get the outcome they desire.

"**The foundation of adaptability is deep curiosity,**" Bobby emphasized. "It's the first of the 7 Tactical Skills of Optimal Mental Performance.

"As an athlete, are you deeply curious about *finding the best way*, or is it only about *getting your way?* Will you *go through* the summer, or will you *grow through* the summer? When adversity hits this summer, will you get frustrated or fascinated?

"The choice is yours. Are you going to be a dying dinosaur or a ferocious Frog?"

Bobby dropped the mic, as our school song blasted from the speakers.

We went wild!

CHAPTER 22
TACTICAL SKILL #1 - DEEP CURIOSITY

With that, the lights in the auditorium turned back on. I had never been so inspired by our four-legged school mascot as I was in that moment.

Coach Whitlock picked up the mic with a smile. "How about that? A mic drop from Bobby Bobsled!" We all applauded again.

"The painted frogs on the sleds are there as a reminder of who we are, adaptable, tough, and extremely curious.

"Deep Curiosity is our #1 Tactical Skill because once you think you know it all, you are finished. Once you think you have arrived, complacency kicks in and catastrophe quickly follows.

"Staying curious allows you to remove judgement and ask better questions.

"Better questions create better answers," she emphasized.

Dr. Caroline Leaf, one of the world's best cognitive neuroscientists says, 'Staying deeply curious will expand your life experience, help you get unstuck, move you forward, create new perspectives, improve your relationships, help you process instead of suppress, and increase your health span and longevity.'

"Today, I'm going to share two drills that will help you build the skill of curiosity. As athletes, we do drills to build skills physically. We must also do drills to build skills mentally. The process is identical."

40

CHAPTER 23
DRILL #1 - THE MVP PROCESS

Coach Whitlock spoke with passion. "The inspiration behind the Separation Through Preparation framework came from my time at the Olympic Training Center. I tailored it for high school athletes.

"I remember my first Winning Edge Wednesday speaker was Brian Cain. He is one of the nation's premier mental performance coaches. Cain introduced a drill that challenged us to use Tactical Skill #1, Deep Curiosity. It's called the MVP Process, which stands for Mission, Vision, and Principles.

"Cain said, 'Get curious, then get serious about defining who you are and what you want to accomplish. When you know your MVP, it becomes easier to get out of bed in the morning and attack the day. If you don't know your MVP, then how you feel that day will determine your actions. If we only relied on our feelings, we would all be sleeping right now.'"

"I'd rather be sleeping right now," chirped Kinger.

"Rather than just talk about it, I wanted you to see my first MVP process. Go to page five in your manual."

Whitlock called on Kinger, who had his hand raised.

"So, if you were just an alternate, your vision didn't exactly work out, did it?" Kinger said.

"Very true. When you have the courage to set an optimistic vision,

M.V.P. PROCESS

NAME: Jess Whitlock

MISSION
I will be remembered as a teammate who:

Works hard every practice, supports teammates even when my practice or performance isn't going well, keeps a positive attitude regardless of how I feel

VISION
My vision is to:

My vision is to be a crew member on the Olympic bobsledding team and represent the United States.

PRINCIPLES
The principles that will guide my mission and vision are:

Honesty – I will follow the team rules on curfew, drugs and alcohol

Open-mindedness – I will listen and apply the feedback from my coaches without taking critisism personally

Accountability – I will own my mistakes and not make excuses when my performance is not up to Olympic standards

SUCCESS
Definition of Success for the Upcoming Season/Year:

Do my absolute best to make the bobsled team and leave nothing behind.

ONE WORD INTENTION:

PRESENCE

one that's not guaranteed, there is a chance you will come up short. That's the risk you take when going after something significant. You've got to be willing to deal with the doubters, haters, and critics. As one of my coaches always said, **the loudest boos come from the cheapest seats**.

"To your point, Kinger, you're right. My vision didn't come true. However, I was blessed to be a part of an Olympic team. And, as I said at our very first meeting, I haven't participated on an official Olympic bobsled race *yet*. Thanks for asking the tough question, Kinger. The tough questions make us reflect and grow."

Kinger seemed at a loss for words, which was a first. All he could do was nod. I had a feeling most of us would face a few tough questions as the summer went on.

"Please find the blank MVP form on page six. All the drills we share will work if you work them. We are not requiring any forms to be handed in to us. It's on you. You decide what you want to accomplish this summer, this school year, and really for the rest of your life. We are recommending that you complete the MVP process tonight. Let's complete the form using the summer as the timeframe. For now, we can leave blank the last box where it reads 'ONE WORD COMMITMENT.' We will cover that later this summer."

A blank M.V.P. Process form is included in the Extra Push section at the end of the book.

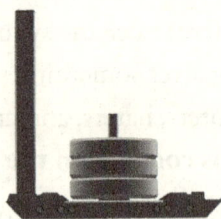

CHAPTER 24
THE SUCCESS CYCLE

"You will also notice we have included blank journal pages in the back of the manual. Use these to press pause and reflect on the last twenty-four hours of your life." We suggest that you do this as part of your routine at the end of the day or after training," Coach Whitlock explained.

"Now, let's look at an important concept called The Success Cycle. Preparing–Performing–Reviewing. This three-part cycle is vital in order to achieve optimal performance.

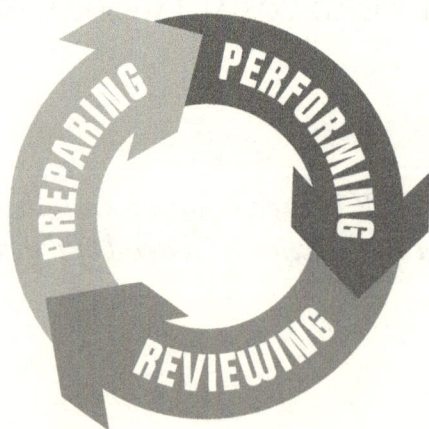

"Most athletes understand the importance of preparing and performing, so that's where most of their energy goes. How many of you watch film of your next opponent?"

Most of us raised our hands.

"How many of you watch film from your previous game or performance?"

Not as many hands went up.

"How many of you don't like watching yourself on film?"

A majority of hands went up.

"I actually like it because I like to see how many kids I juked out," said the arrogant Kinger as he turned to me. "How about you, Jackson? Have you watched the final play YET?"

I hated how he used Whitlock's 'yet' idea against me. I felt my face turn red in anger, but I managed to keep my mouth shut. *What a jerk,* I thought.

"What was that, Kinger?" asked Whitlock.

"Nothing, just telling Jackson how I agree with you. It's important to watch film," Kinger replied with a smirk.

She took a long pause, like she knew Kinger wasn't telling the truth, then continued, "For most of us, watching ourselves on film can be painful because what we see in our head doesn't always match what's on the screen. It's frustrating when we know what we *want* to look and perform like, then the video shows what we *actually* look and perform like. It's humbling. Agreed?"

Almost all our heads nodded.

"During our Olympic training sessions, we spent hours watching film. Our coaches would dial in on the smallest details. Early on, I remember getting defensive. Sometimes, I would shut down mentally and just nod my head even though I was zoned out. The breakthrough for me happened during a Winning Edge Wednesday when the guest speaker said something profound. **The best athletes in the world seek the feedback without the pushback.**

"A small pocket of athletes understand the incredible power of reviewing. When done right, it can significantly help future performances."

CHAPTER 25
DRILL #2 - WELL-BETTER-HOW

"Drill #2 is called Well–Better–How. These three simple questions will help you with the most overlooked part of the success cycle: reviewing. Before we dive into them, let's discuss the difference between reliving and reviewing."

Whitlock pointed to Olivia. "Olivia, what do you think the difference is between reliving and reviewing?"

"I think reviewing is more like it's in the past. Reliving makes it feel like it's still happening now," she replied.

"Nicely put. Too many times we are guilty of reliving a past mistake instead of reviewing a past mistake. Reliving a mistake can bring up the same feelings and emotions as it did when we made it. When our brain starts seeing the mistake being replayed, we are more likely to repeat the mistake."

What Whitlock said to my sister reminded me of the conversation I had with Bobby at the field the other night. I knew I needed to quit reliving the last play but, for some reason, I just couldn't.

"We are going to challenge you to take a few minutes at the end of your day to complete a Well–Better–How form."

Coach Whitlock turned on the projector.

She went on to break down each question. "What did I do well today? Looking at what you did well builds momentum for the next day.

"Next question, what could I have done better? No one is perfect. We all mess up. Think back to your interactions with the people you crossed paths with today. Think about your effort and attitude. What situations could you have done better?

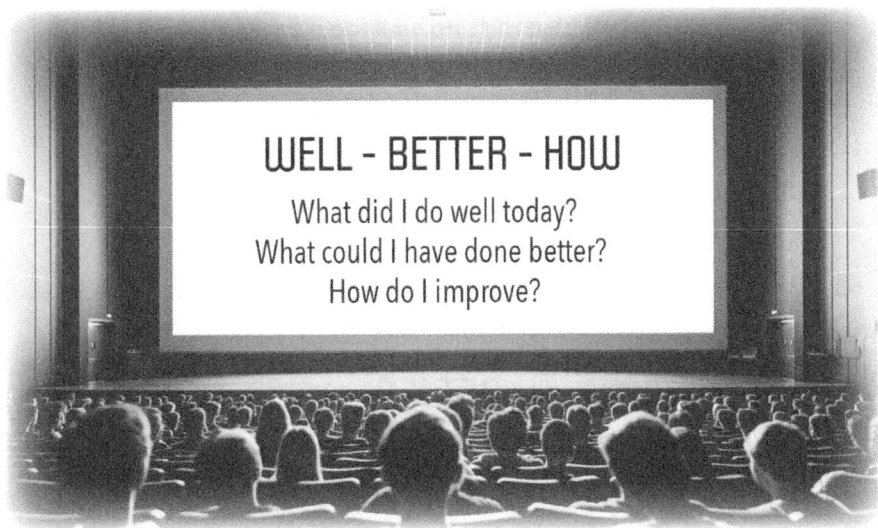

"Final question, how do I improve? Knowledge minus action equals nothing. What action do you need to take to improve for next time? Do you need to talk to, not text, someone to clear up a misunderstanding? Do you need to change your attitude or effort at home, in class, or in your sport? Do you need to put in more preparation?"

I never asked myself these questions. This was good stuff.

Whitlock stated, "This process can be difficult at first because it forces us to take a serious look at our performance. Once it becomes a habit, you will become comfortable and see the value of reviewing your day instead of reliving your day. Give yourselves three claps, on three. One, two, three."

"That wraps up the first Mental Performance Monday. Do you know what time it is now? Game time!" Coach Whitlock showed a diagram of the field, the flow of workouts, and a list of teams.

WELL - BETTER - HOW

WELL
What did I do well today?

BETTER
What could I have done better?

HOW
How do I improve?

CHAPTER 26
BOAT CREWS

"Each team of fifteen athletes will be known as a boat crew. This is a borrowed term from Navy SEAL BUD/S training. That stands for Basic Underwater Demolition/SEALs training, in which our nation's best defenders would be put on small teams. They carry two-hundred-pound rafts in and out of the ocean followed by endless physical drills in the sand, all while hardly sleeping for an entire week. What some of you might call a tough morning of training would be a joke to them. While our workouts couldn't hold a candle to SEAL training, we admire the spirit of what SEALs stand for. We want you to model the SEAL mindset as you work together as a small team and then later as a large group."

We hustled out of the auditorium. Once on the field, we quickly found our groups and stations. The scoreboard read *Period 1 10:00*. We heard Coach Whitlock's voice over the PA system as she counted "Three... two... one... GO!"

All the boat crews were made up of athletes from various sports with various levels of strength and experience. Some of the senior athletes on my boat crew included Jamal, who played soccer; Grace, from the lacrosse team; and Taylor, a top-ranked volleyball player in the state of Minnesota. This was a cool way to have different sports be on the same team.

Having a variety of sports on my boat crew made me suddenly realize that I wasn't very good about showing up to support other sports.

That was something to write in the *Better* box tonight.

Each crew was asked to select a captain and two assistant leaders. My crew chose me as captain, and Jamal and Grace were named assistant leaders.

Each team would push and pull the sled, while the other members of the boat crew did body weight exercises. It was competitive, organized, and super fun.

Every ten minutes, Bobby Bobsled would blow his whistle, and the boat crew captain or assistant leader would run to him and get instruction on the next set of exercises. Then they would sprint back to their boat crews to relay the workout.

"Player-led, not coach-fed," was the focus for the day, Bobby would say.

After the workout, Bobby called up all the boat crew leaders and assistants and went through a short Well–Better–How discussion.

It seemed like the coaches weren't just talking about drills and skills from Monday, we were actually doing them.

It was quite different from what we had done in the past. We were outside on the fields, not just in the weight room or running a mile on the track. Coaches focused on technique rather than just carelessly counting reps. Plus, the bumpin' music was something totally new.

As we walked to the parking lot, naysayers did what naysayers do.

Kinger and Olivia complained about the style of music, being outside in the heat, and having to work out with other people not in their sport. Surprisingly, they now missed last year, where the standards were low and the supervision was light.

Coach Whitlock was much more organized and juiceful than Coach Johnson. I liked it and couldn't wait to come back.

CHAPTER 27
NOT ON BOARD

Tuesday, we were all on the field at 6:00. The two-hour workout included a warmup that felt like a full workout, followed by speed and agility drills and sled work as the finisher.

Whitlock asked all ten captains and twenty assistant leaders to meet at the fifty-yard line. Then she dropped the news.

"Tomorrow, I need all of you in the auditorium at 5:30 for additional leadership training before the first Winning Edge Wednesday."

I was cool with it, but on the walk to the parking lot a handful of boat crew leaders and assistants, including Kinger and Olivia, were far from cool with it.

"Five-thirty in the morning, are you kidding me? Six o'clock is early enough," Kinger complained.

"Why do I have to be a boat crew captain? I shouldn't have to tell people what to do. That's a coach's job," Olivia said.

I wanted to remind them that Bobby had told us the summer program would shift from being coach-fed to player-led, but I decided to keep the thought to myself and see how things played out.

CHAPTER 28
LEADERSHIP

The 5:00 alarm came awfully fast. For the third day in a row, I was up before the sun came up.

"Mornin'," Coach Whitlock said as she entered the auditorium, already sweating from her early morning workout.

"Morning," we echoed back, rather quietly.

"Nothing wakes you up like pushing the sled before sunup. Bobby and some of the staff were already getting after it this morning. If we want you to do it, we must do it ourselves," Coach Whitlock said.

"Leaders live it, and you are the leaders in the school. That's why you were selected yesterday. Leadership isn't easy, it isn't always fun, and it isn't for everyone. However, being a good leader is a trainable skill. Too often, athletes are put in a position of leadership because of their physical skills. **Leadership is a behavior—not a position.** It's part of our goal this summer to help educate, empower, and energize you to be the best athlete and leader you can be.

"Like any other skill, to get better at leadership, you need to get reps in. Keep in mind there are some team leaders who are not team captains, and there are some team captains who are not team leaders. Let's not get locked into thinking you have to be named team captain to be considered a team leader."

CHAPTER 29
STANDARDS > SCOREBOARD

Coach Whitlock went on, "As leaders, we want to start competing to a standard, not a scoreboard."

Olivia raised her hand and said, "I don't get it. What's that even mean? Every sport is different, and some sports don't have a scoreboard." She put air quotes around "scoreboard."

Who uses air quotes anymore? I thought.

Bobby Bobsled jumped in and seemed unaffected by my sister's negative tone. "Good question, Olivia. **Competing to a scoreboard focuses on the question *'did we win?'***

"Hey, I like to win. You don't get to be an Olympic athlete if you're okay with losing. To this day, I try to win in everything I do. Heck, I time myself mowing the lawn hoping to reach a new PR!"

Kinger appreciated this comment and said, "Nice one, Coach."

Bobby smiled and continued, **"Competing to a standard focuses on the question *'how did we perform?'*** This helps us focus on the process, not just the outcome. In sports, a standard is created by hitting proven targets that show you have the best chance to win. This is based on overall averages.

"For example, in baseball or softball, the first run wins seventy percent of the time. In football, the team who wins the turnover battle wins seventy percent of the time, too. In tennis, if you lose the first set in a three-set match, only twenty-two percent of the time does that player win the next two. Of course, if you don't hit the target, you can still come back and win. It's the bounce that counts. Hitting the standards doesn't guarantee success either. But you are trying to get on the right side of the law of averages, because the law of averages is always at work.

"In sports, the law of averages means one of four things is going to happen." Bobby clicked the remote and the screen lit up.

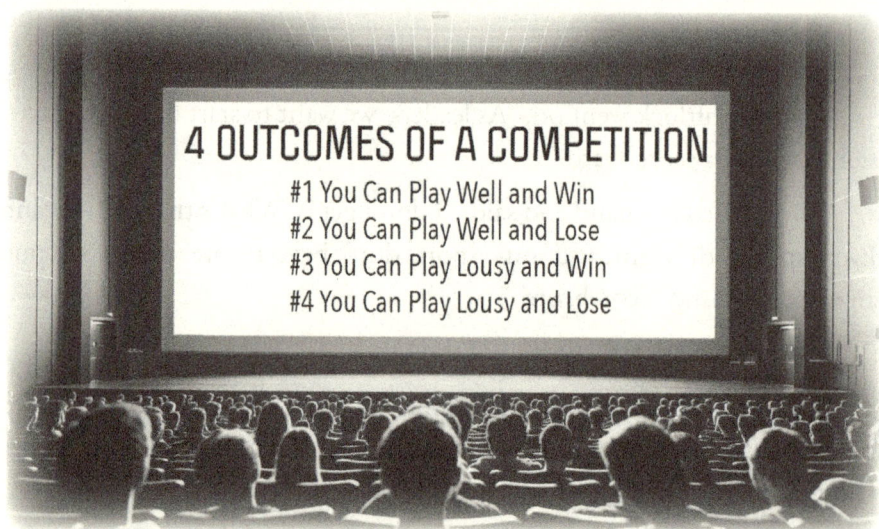

4 OUTCOMES OF A COMPETITION
#1 You Can Play Well and Win
#2 You Can Play Well and Lose
#3 You Can Play Lousy and Win
#4 You Can Play Lousy and Lose

"As Olivia pointed out, standards will vary from sport to sport. Standards for a cheer squad will obviously be different than standards for a lacrosse team. Once you figure this out for yourself and for your team, you will gain a competitive advantage.

"If you play well and win but didn't notice and identify how and why you performed well, how will you know how to repeat it for the next game?

"It's like having the ingredients for a cake in front of you but no idea how much of each ingredient is needed or the sequence to mixing them together. You're basically crossing your fingers and hoping you're lucky enough to get an amazing result.

"In bobsledding, every aspect of the entire run had a specific standard. Our coaches measured the smallest details, right down to the distance between each step before launching ourselves into the sled. Everything you can imagine was measured. Everything made a difference. The difference between a gold medal and a silver medal is 0.026 of a second!

"Coach Whitlock and I will be talking with each of your head coaches about determining the targets for success during your season. When you hit the targets, you tend to get the best results."

"Our standard is internal. It's what we create and agree to abide by. It's not based on other people, external circumstances, and things outside of our control."

Coach Bobby showed us a new slide. "The six standards we are targeting this summer include:

SUMMER STANDARDS
Be on Time
Bring the Juice
Do What's Right
Encourage +Support Each Other
Control What You Can Control
Do the Work

"Whether it's in sports or in life, if you adhere to these six standards, you start closing the gap from where you are to where you want to be," Bobby Bobsled said. "Coach Whitlock will take it from here."

CHAPTER 30
SLED JACKS

"Moving forward, each Wednesday morning from 5:30 to 6:00, boat crew captains along with assistant leaders will be a part of leadership training and development. We will have a variety of discussions, strategies, and activities that will enhance your ability to lead this summer.

"This morning, we will hustle across the hall to the gym to rehearse sled jacks, a fundamental piece of the Separation Through Preparation program. Then we will listen to our guest speaker, who will kick off our first Winning Edge Wednesday. After the speaker wraps up, we will head out to the fields for physical training.

"Just like the success cycle we covered on Monday, we want you to be prepared to lead your boat crews to perform. Sound good?" Whitlock asked.

She got a few nods from us, but not a loud YES.

"Here's how sled jacks work," Whitlock explained. She and Bobby divided us into three groups of ten. We lined up in three rows.

Bobby gave the instructions. "First order is to get order. We need perfect rows." A few people shifted in line.

"Nice work. This is how we will start each rep," Bobby explained. "Pay attention, because you will be accountable for repeating what we do here when we get outside. As the Navy SEALs say, everything rises and falls on leadership."

Bobby asked me to be the leader of the leaders. When I stood in front of the three rows, all eyes were on me.

"Jackson, as team leader, you will give the opening command by yelling 'Sled Jacks!' Boat crew members, you will call back, 'Sled Jacks!' You will then say 'Ready,' and they will echo back 'Ready.' You will then say 'Push,' and they will respond with 'The Sled.' Does everyone get that? Let's practice it."

Team Leader: "Sled Jacks"

Teammates: "Sled Jacks"

Team Leader: "Ready"

Teammates: "Ready"

Team Leader: "Push"

Teammates: "The Sled"

After about ten reps, we finally got the cadence down. The key for me was to remember my role and responsibility. I only said the team leader command. Sometimes I messed up and forgot my commands. Other times I said what the team said.

Now we were ready for the next set of instructions from Bobby.

"Okay, once your boat crew says, 'The Sled,' the action starts. Jackson, you will count out in a loud voice, 'One... two... three.' After three, all of you will start the first of eight jumping jacks in unison. The standard for a jumping jack is that your hands clap together at the top with your feet apart, and then you slap your thighs at the bottom with your ankles touching each other. After the second jumping jack, you and your boat crew will shout the letter S. We will follow that cadence and spell S-L-E-D after every other jumping jack. So, the boat crews yell the letters of S-L-E-D after jumping jacks two, four, six, and eight. At the end of spelling S-L-E-D, Jackson will shout out, 'Integrity!'

"If anyone is out of sync with the jumping jacks, doesn't meet the standard, or says the wrong letter or word, they will have an opportunity to raise their hand and acknowledge how they messed up. After all integrity comments have been shared, Jackson will ask for two claps, and you will yell 'Next!' in unison. Let's give it a try!"

Getting thirty people in three rows to do eight jumping jacks in perfect unison sounded easy, but it wasn't. I found a new appreciation for cheerleaders and the dance line. I called myself on integrity at least five times before I got my part right. Almost every member of my boat crew called themselves on an integrity violation except Kinger and Olivia.

I couldn't believe it took us twenty minutes to put together a perfect set. It was now 6:00 and time to return to the auditorium for our guest speaker.

CHAPTER 31
1% BETTER

"CHECK IN!" said Coach Whitlock.

"ALL IN!" the athletes replied as they took their seats in the auditorium.

"This is the first of our Winning Edge Wednesday. The goal is to help and challenge everyone one in this room, including me and the coaches, to become our best.

"Please take out your training manuals and turn to page five for your first guest speaker," Coach Whitlock instructed. "Our first speaker today is Mr. Joe Bigsby. You may have seen him subbing at the high school. What you may not know is Mr. Bigsby is a Minnesota coaching legend. In the nineties, he coached six different teams to a state championship. Ten years ago, he was inducted into the Minnesota Coaches Hall of Fame. His enthusiasm for coaching and life are contagious. Join me in a warm welcome for Mr. Bigsby."

Despite his impressive resume, the round of applause at that hour of the morning wasn't real impressive.

"Thank you, Coach Whitlock. It's a pleasure to be here today," Mr. Bigsby said. "I have had many of you in the classroom while subbing here at Pine Lake. I must tell you how impressed I am that you're here so early today.

"I've been preparing to deliver today's talk for weeks. Ferocious Frogs,

I don't take today's message lightly. I'm here on purpose with a purpose!" Bigsby belted with enthusiasm.

"During my thirty-two year career teaching and coaching in a different district, I saw a ton of physically talented athletes come and go. I saw students who had incredible athletic ability, but their mental game was below average. They were uncoachable. When things didn't go their way, they would fall apart.

"On the other hand, I saw athletes who recognized they had average or even below average talent. In order to compete, they had to outwork everyone. What they didn't have in talent, they made up for with effort. Then they doubled down on their mental game and went on to have a stellar high school career. Many of them went on to have excellent college careers as well.

"Maybe some of you weren't gifted with amazing physical talent. You still have the ability to contribute and compete and make a name for yourself by outworking those who have more talent. Talent may get you in the door. But, your attitude and effort determine how long you will stay.

"Look, every school has a summer weightlifting program. The question is what are you doing to separate yourselves from your competition?"

After a long pause, Mr. Bigsby said, "One percent of your day. That doesesn't sound like much does it? Well, that's fourteen minutes and twenty-four seconds. What would happen if you dedicated just one percent of your day around a specific area you either want to or need to improve on? What if you did this consistently with focus and energy for a year?

"In the short term, improving by just one percent is hardly noticeable, however, the long-term results are quite notable. Check out the graph on page five. This is from James Clear's amazing book *Atomic Habits*. One of my all-time favorite books that has literally changed my life.

"Little by little, a little becomes a lot is not just a cute phrase on a wristband. It's real! **When you get one percent better each day for a year, you'll end up thirty-seven times better than when you started.**

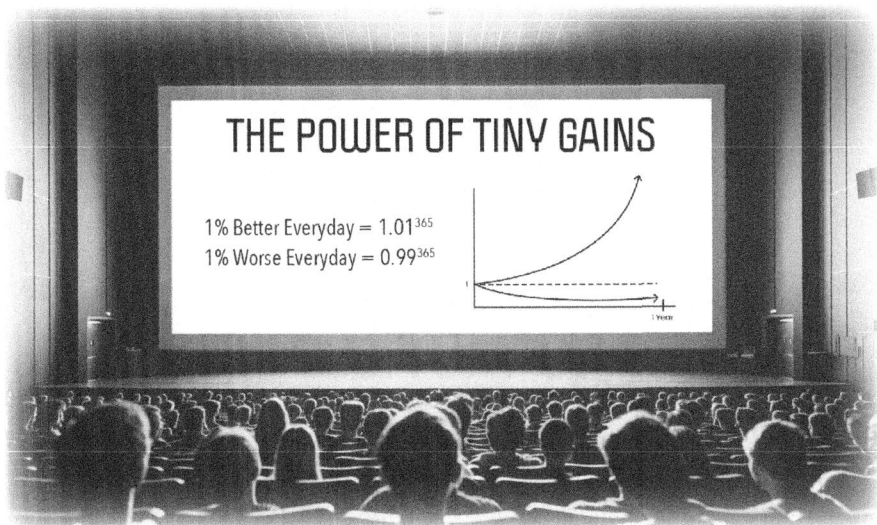

THE POWER OF TINY GAINS

1% Better Everyday = 1.01^{365}
1% Worse Everyday = 0.99^{365}

"What are you going to do intentionally with your fourteen minutes and twenty-four seconds to get closer to being the person and athlete you want to be? You now have a chance to design your one percent game plan in your manual."

I wrote, *daily footwork drills to improve my drop back steps for our passing plays.*

Mr. Bigsby wrapped up his talk with the little-known fact, "Frogs can't jump backward. They can only jump forward. Let's embrace the Ferocious Frog mentality by jumping forward and commit to improving one percent better every single day."

The applause from a hundred and fifty students at the end of his talk was impressive by Pine Lake standards. Bigsby was on fire. I had no idea he was so inspirational.

Scan the QR Code to watch how to get 1% better every day by James Clear

CHAPTER 32
TO THE FIELD

After Mr. Bigsby talked about getting one percent better, the ten captains and twenty assistant captains from the boat crews were invited on stage to demonstrate how a successful sled jack looked. This time we were able to nail it after only five attempts. Next, we headed to the field and got into our boat crews to practice the sled jacks.

My boat crew had an integrity violation on every attempt. After several minutes, Coach Whitlock brought all one hundred fifty of us together to test our ability to work as a large group. Unfortunately, we never completed a perfect sled jack together. Throughout the entire set of sled jacks, all I could see was that Olivia and Kinger were not holding themselves to the standard.

When we finished the workout, crew captains and assistant leaders stayed and debriefed with Coach Whitlock, using the Well–Better–How method. We learned the results from group to group were similar. Boat crew members would occasionally hold themselves to the standard but would rarely hold a teammate to the standard.

"That's normal," Coach Whitlock explained. "But, normal will get you beat. Normal is being alright with average effort. Normal is being more concerned with being popular than doing what's right and meeting the standard.

"If you want to be a leader and have a season of significance, you must hold yourself to the standard first. Then you can hold your teammates to that same standard.

"I noticed that most of you were willing to call 'integrity' on yourself when you didn't meet a standard. But I didn't hear anyone call 'integrity' on another crew member when they would miss the standard.

"Leadership can be uncomfortable and challenging. Calling 'integrity' on ourselves is uncomfortable because no one wants to look stupid in front of their peers. Calling 'integrity' on others is challenging for kids and adults because we don't want to be seen as the boss of anyone and put our friendship on the line.

"Back in Utah, our Olympic coaches challenged us to shift our mindset from *calling out* to *calling up*. Calling out is about making someone look bad. Calling up is about raising others up to our standard. Often, it means giving instructions on how to do something right. As difficult as this may be, let's start to create a culture where we are willing to call ourselves and others up. If we can create this type of culture, we have the potential to become better than we have ever been!

"Sometimes a simple pocket phrase like, 'That's not the Frog way,' is a great cue to help your teammates refocus and get back on the right track.

"Today was a decent start. I've seen worse. We'll get better. Leadership is a process, not an event.

"Let's huddle up and get a breakdown. Left hands in because they are closer to your heart, palms up so we can lift each other up. Frogs on three. One-two-three!"

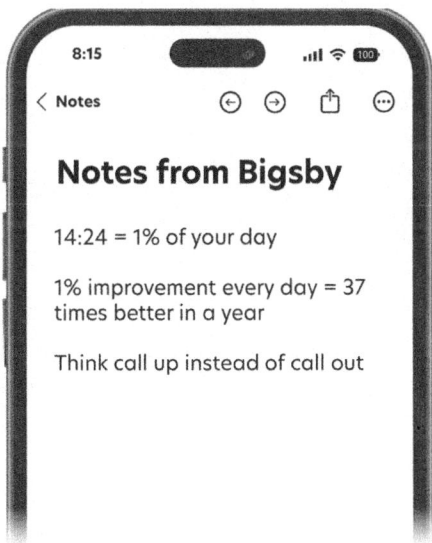

8:15

< Notes

Notes from Bigsby

14:24 = 1% of your day

1% improvement every day = 37 times better in a year

Think call up instead of call out

"FROGS!" we yelled together as we broke.

Walking back to the parking lot, I felt like I had learned a few leadership lessons and created a new note on my phone.

Who knew how much could be learned from doing jumping jacks?

CHAPTER 33
THE END OF WEEK ONE

Thursday meant the last day of training for the week. I was tired and sore, which wasn't surprising for the first week.

Not only was I being challenged physically and mentally, but I was also being challenged as the captain of my boat crew. The upside was I felt like I had developed more as a leader in the past four days than I had all last year.

I was also one of a few athletes who would show up for the optional Champions Do More afternoon sled workouts. If leaders 'live it' like Bobby and Coach Whitlock said, then **optional wasn't optional for me.** If I expected my teammates to be all in, then as a senior, and as a captain, I had to show them I was all in.

I was shocked that we were a hundred and fifty strong every morning for the first four days. That was better attendance than we had ever had in the past.

I was also consistently journaling my Well–Better–How reflections at the end of each day.

It was fun getting to know kids from different sports who were in my boat crew. I had to admit, I unfairly judged some of them before actually getting to know them. Even though I didn't like being judged, I could sometimes fall into the trap of being judgmental.

I was enjoying it.

Olivia, on the other hand, not so much.

"If I have to do any more sled jacks or push that stupid sled, I'm going to lose it," she complained to me over and over.

I laughed and wanted to say, "You can't lose it if you never had it." But with Olivia, I had learned that sometimes it was better to say nothing at all and let her do her thing.

I was very curious to see what Coach Whitlock and Bobby Bobsled had in store for next week. But first, it was time to bash.

CHAPTER 34
TACTICAL SKILL #2 - FOCUS & AWARENESS

The weekend bash at the beach was fun, even though there were fewer people than last week. The summer was flying by. I couldn't believe it was already the third week of June.

"CHECK IN!" Bobby shouted as he lowered the welcome music in the auditorium.

"ALL IN!" we replied. It seemed like we had lost some of our enthusiasm from last week.

"I hope you had a nice weekend. Today's Mental Performance Monday will cover Tactical Skill #2 of Optimal Mental Performance; Focus and Awareness.

"Focus and awareness are essential in life and sports. **Your focus determines your future.** Being aware of our focus level is the first step to all growth and improvement."

Bobby took a large magnifying glass off the podium. "Imagine taking this magnifying glass outside on a sunny summer day in Minnesota. If you face the glass to the ground but constantly shift it around every few seconds, the magnifying glass has no impact. But if you hold the magnifying glass in place and focus the sun's rays through it, soon the channeled energy will create enough heat to literally start a fire. Your performance is the same way. If you can channel your focus and energy on what's important to you, you can stay fired up and aligned with your MVP process. Those who constantly shift their focus rarely find that their MVP becomes real."

Bobby continued, "Top performers are extremely aware that they may have to say no to some choices or events that could distract them from achieving their goals. Often, those missed moments are captured on social media by friends who may have invited you to join in. This can magnify the feeling of missing out on life. Perhaps you've looked at social media and thought, 'Compared to everyone else, my life stinks!' Has that happened to anyone?"

Almost all the hands went up.

"Social media is not always accurate. Most photos that are posted to social tend to be a way to say, 'Look at me! My life is awesome!'

"Let's be aware of our Mission, Vision, and Principles. We have to focus on what we focus on.

"The next two drills Coach Whitlock has for today will help you increase your focus and awareness as you work on making the MVP process become a reality," he concluded.

CHAPTER 35
DRILL #3 – CONCENTRATION GRIDS

"Please turn to page seven of your training manual. You will find a seven-by-seven grid with forty-nine numbers randomly entered in each grid block," Coach Whitlock said.

47	24	10	15	40	27	23
11	07	13	37	43	00	12
32	21	19	38	17	29	36
33	45	04	28	42	48	20
41	30	09	26	18	03	14
44	34	02	05	22	01	06
25	35	08	39	16	46	31

"When I say 'go,' you will start by crossing off zero, then one, then two, and so on in succession until you get to forty-nine. When you're done, look at the timer on the screen. Be honest, and jot down your finish time. **Measurement creates motivation.** You can't improve on what you don't measure. Let's compete and see how well you can focus. Three... two... one... GO!"

I was only halfway done, and Kinger was saying random numbers in my ear just to mess with me.

This drill was a lot tougher than I thought it would be. It was embarrassing as the starting quarterback and team captain to take so long in such a simple drill. It also didn't help that I heard Olivia say, "Done," as she finished first. I was one of the last ones to finish.

I'd like to blame my late finish on Kinger being a jerk, but it was on me.

Whitlock asked us to jot down the lessons from the concentration grid in our manual. Then a few athletes shared their ideas out loud.

A wrestler said, "I finally started to get in a groove when I figured out instead of just putting a single line through the number I was on it worked better to completely block it out. That way the square was no longer appeared an option."

A track athlete jumped in. "I realized I should only focus on the current number I was searching for and not get ahead of myself. One time, I was trying to remember where number twenty was located when I needed to find number fifteen."

For me, this concentration grid made me realize that I need to focus on completing one play at a time.

CHAPTER 36
DRILL #4 – ONE WORD COMMITMENT

"Go back to your MVP process form. There's a One-Word Commitment box at the bottom we asked you to leave blank until today.

"I'm curious, what's one word that represents what you stand for this summer? What's one word that you are committed to living this summer to help you get the results that you really want? What's the one word you need to be reminded of when it's ninety-five degrees and you're on the field pushing the sled?" Whitlock asked.

As Whitlock called on us to share, some of the words that were thrown out included: "Faster," "Discipline," "Joy," "Work," "Focus," "Stronger."

As I sat there still staring at my concentration grid, my one-word commitment hit me.

I raised my hand and said, "Presence" in a confident tone.

The coaches then gave a bunch of markers to the athletes who sat at each aisle.

"Even though you'll all use a permanent marker to write your one-word commitment on your wristband, chances are the word will rub off every day. When it does, you *get to* re-write and recommit to your one-word commitment," Whitlock said. **Every day, you get to set your intention about how you want to show up.** Writing and rewriting on the band sends a message to the brain that you are intentional, aware, and focused on

71

your Mission, Vision, and Principles.

"To improve your focus and awareness, you need to be where your feet are. It's one step, or in the case of a concentration grid, one number at a time. Now, let's concentrate on today's physical workout," an inspired Whitlock responded as the workout appeared on the screen.

After Whitlock finished Mental Performance Monday, we bolted from the auditorium to the field for a sixty-minute intense workout.

Tuesday's workout was no picnic either, with plyo stations, core exercises, and of course, sled work.

CHAPTER 37
DRILL # 5 THE SUCCESS CHECKLIST

All boat crew captains and assistant captains were on the stage floor at 5:30 for the second leadership training before the large group Winning Edge Wednesday session.

Whitlock asked us to reflect on our first year at Pine Lake and describe the qualities of a junior or senior leader we admired. Most of the stories, including mine, were about older students who went out of their way to make the younger students feel welcome. Interestingly enough, none of the stories talked about the leader's athletic ability in their given sport. She closed the training with a question. "If I ask the same question two years from now, will someone tell a story about you?"

At 5:55, Coach Whitlock hit the music, and the doors opened. After everyone was seated, she took the mic.

"Frogs, we have an incredible guest speaker today. He's one of the biggest boosters of PLHS athletics, a former coach at the University of Minnesota, and a successful businessperson in the area. He has a reputation for working hard and having a great sense of humor.

"Let's give a thunderous round of applause for Mr. Mike Daxter!"

"Thanks for the invitation, Coach Whitlock. Most of you didn't even know my first name was Mike! Everyone just calls me Dax.

"Coach Whitlock made me feel a part of what you are doing this summer by giving me one of the wristbands that you have been rocking." He raised his arm to show his wrist.

"LBL. 'Little by little, a little becomes'… what?"

"A lot!" we said as a large group.

"Dax right!" Dax said, raising his eyebrows and laughing at his own dad joke.

"Beautiful. I love catchy phrases! I have a mental bank of them so I can withdraw them at the right time." Dax smirked.

"Here's a catchy phrase to jot down in your manuals. **'Things that are easy to do are easy not to do.'** I've found the best way to get myself to do the things I know are good for me is to keep a success checklist. After using it for a few months, I have noticed my success checklist keeps me in alignment with my mission, vision, and principles. This simple checklist helps me handle the little things so I can handle the big things like run several projects, manage over a hundred employees, and attend every family event. Once I started using this strategy consistently, distractions were no longer a problem.

"This approach has changed my life, and that's why Coach Whitlock asked me to introduce Drill #5, The Success Checklist.

"This summer, your coaches have introduced some new skills and training drills. I know, because my daughter comes home and tells me all about it. I'll try not to embarrass her with a dad joke or a story about her childhood. Faith, please stand up for a second."

Faith, a junior, played volleyball and basketball, stood up and waved to everyone with a big smile. With her personal success, combined with her family's successes, she could easily have been arrogant. But she wasn't. She carried herself with a humble confidence.

"Most of you know Faith. We named her that because we had *faith* she would do well in life. Sorry, I couldn't help myself," joked Dax.

He continued, "In our house, it's mandatory that all of us create and use a success checklist. Faith, I'll stop embarrassing you if you can share four items on your morning checklist."

She took out her phone, scrolled for a few seconds, and said, "My morning checklist starts the night before, because I'm not much of a morning person. Before going to sleep, I put out what I'm going to wear the next day, so I'm not rushed. If I didn't do this, I would just stare at my closet each morning.

"So, here's my morning list. First, I make my bed. Second, I listen to a short podcast while stretching. Third, I do ten push-ups, twenty sit-ups, and thirty air squats before breakfast. Then I drink my bottle of water and fill it back up before heading to school."

She smiled and nodded at her dad before she sat back down. Dax's face made it clear that he was proud of her. *What parent wouldn't be?* I thought.

He continued, "Thanks, Faith. Now, would you all agree those four things are easy to do?"

Heads nodded.

"But they are also easy to...what?"

"Not to do," we replied.

"It's the start that stops most people. A success checklist won't work unless you work it. You must create the list or you won't be motivated to follow it. Remember, measurement creates motivation. Our family uses the free app, HabitShare. You can use pen and paper if that works for you. Whether it's crossing off an item on paper or clicking 'complete' on your phone, you

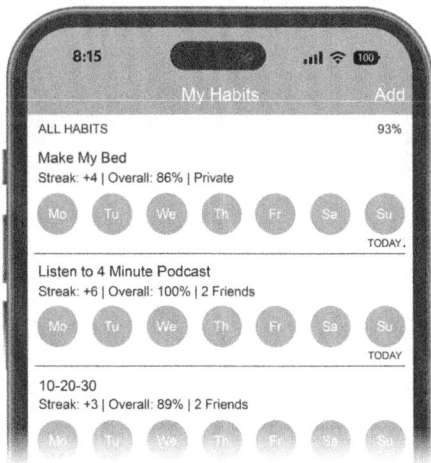

8:15

My Habits   Add

ALL HABITS   93%

Make My Bed
Streak: +4 | Overall: 86% | Private

Mo Tu We Th Fr Sa Su
TODAY

Listen to 4 Minute Podcast
Streak: +6 | Overall: 100% | 2 Friends

Mo Tu We Th Fr Sa Su
TODAY

10-20-30
Streak: +3 | Overall: 89% | 2 Friends

Mo Tu We Th Fr Sa Su

create momentum in life by winning each day, one day at a time. By the way, making your bed is a non-negotiable item on all the Daxters' checklists."

"Let's start right now by getting the app and creating options for our morning routine," said Daxter.

As HabitShare started to download on my phone, I realized I didn't have a solid morning routine. I had been doing some of the same things as Faith, but I wasn't keeping track or giving myself credit. I typed in everything that Faith said on my checklist, except make my bed. That didn't make sense to me. *Why would I make my bed when I'm just going to crawl back in it at night?* I asked myself.

I added one more item in the weekly section of my success checklist: "FD." Faith Daxter... I was impressed with her presence, and I wanted to get to know her better.

"Remember, it's the start that stops most people. The skills I shared today are easy to do and they are easy not to do. Well, *Dax* about it. So, let's get after it today, Frogs!" He sounded as if he was still coaching college ball.

We all clapped and cheered for Dax as he walked off the stage.

Scan the QR Code to
Download the Habit Share App

CHAPTER 38
SLED CIRCUIT

Wednesday's workout followed a similar flow to last week. Our warm-up started with ten minutes of sled jacks to generate some teamwork.

Coach Bobby then divided us in half and took five of the boat crews to push and pull the sleds.

Coach Whitlock had the other five boat crews work through body weight exercises like squats, flutter kicks, mountain climbers, and push-ups that had to be done in unison.

I could feel some of the frustration building in a lot of the athletes because we struggled to do the body weight exercises in unison.

"Get curious, not furious. **Become fascinated, not frustrated,**" Coach Whitlock reminded all of us.

CHAPTER 39
END OF WEEK TWO

I was determined to continue my streak of doing more. I showed up to the field later in the day for the "Champions Do More" workout, which included sled sprints. I hoped to see Faith Daxter, but she wasn't there. *Maybe she did them earlier in the day.*

More of my football teammates were there than the previous week. I think making the success checklist on HabitShare increased everyone's focus and awareness. Even though there wasn't a coach there, we still warmed up with some Sled Jacks, hoping to be able to pull off a set to the standard. The standard was high, and we weren't there yet.

Although it was only two weeks into the Separation Through Preparation training, I had gained strength, felt more confident, and I even looked bigger. I was also more aware of what it meant to be a leader.

I hoped Olivia and Kinger would get into it more than they were. All I ever heard them talk about was how they wished Coach Johnson was here and that this mental performance stuff was stupid.

I was also concerned because they were starting to hang out a lot. They seemed to always be together at workouts, the beach, or at our house. Kinger was the last person I thought my sister would be into. I guess who she dated wasn't really any of my business, and she would be the first to tell me that, and the second, and the third.

CHAPTER 40
TACTICAL SKILL #3 – PROCESS
OUTCOME

"CHECK IN!" Coach Whitlock said.

"ALL IN!" we replied.

"Inspect what you expect. Please share your success checklists from last week with your boat crew members," she instructed.

As we met in our boat crews, I opened my HabitShare app. When Maurice saw a bunch of red circles next to one item he asked, "Dude, what the heck is FD and why haven't you done it?"

I quickly covered by saying, "Oh, that stands for Footwork Drills for quarterbacks. I do them in my back yard."

"So, why haven't you done them?" he questioned.

I hadn't been tracking that because it really meant talk to Faith. It was the only incomplete task on my success checklist.

"I'm on that this week," I said, trying not to look embarrassed.

After we connected and inspected what we expected with our boat crew members, it was time for us to continue the Mental Performance Monday for week three.

Coach Whitlock announced, "Today we are talking about Tactical Skill

#3 of Optimal Mental Performance, which is Process Over Outcome.

"You have probably heard coaches say, 'trust the process,' but you can't trust the process if you don't have one. Frogs, show me the process that you trust. Please hold up your Habit Share checklist on your phone.

"Trusting the process is like using a staircase. You can't climb the whole staircase all at once. You must take it one step at a time. Today's workout will reinforce that idea."

CHAPTER 41

DRILL #6 - POWER THROUGH PHRASES

Bobby took the stage holding an ancient-looking toolbox. "As you all know, the main reason I was invited to Minnesota this summer was to help Coach Whitlock's fixer-upper house. The other day, I looked in this antique toolbox my father left me when he passed. Inside was this old-school hand drill."

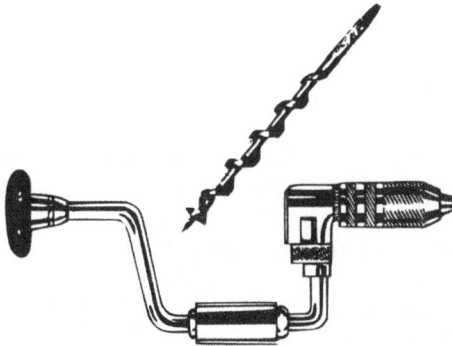

Bobby pulled a thick piece of wood from the toolbox with the word ADVERSITY written on it in black marker. "Olivia, would you be opposed to joining me on stage?" She shook her head no and joined Bobby.

"We are going to do a simple exercise. Olivia, you have thirty seconds to drill as many holes as you can through this ADVERSITY block." Bobby demonstrated how the hand drill worked and then pulled out a stopwatch from his pocket.

Oliva drilled three holes. "Nice job!" said Bobby. We all clapped for her.

Bobby then pulled out a yellow DeWalt drill. "Let's try it one more time using a power drill." Bobby pulled the drill's trigger and the drill bit spun rapidly.

Olivia smiled and said, "That's more like it." Using the power drill, Olivia was able to drill twelve holes.

"So, three holes on the first try and twelve on the second. That's four times the results in the same time period.

Maybe all those home improvement shows Olivia and my mom can't get enough of finally paid off. I thought.

"Which attempt was more enjoyable?"

"Easy, the second one."

"How come?"

"The first time was a lot of work for only three holes. The power drill was fun, and I was able to get more done in the same amount of time."

Bobby grabbed the ADVERSITY block and hand drill. "We are all going to come face-to-face with adversity blocks in life and sports. We can either be like this hand drill tool and grind our way through it," Bobby said as he switched to the DeWalt drill, "or we reach for a power drill and get to the other side in a faster and more efficient way."

"Now, how about a round of applause for Olivia?" We clapped as she returned to her seat.

"Today's drill is called Power Through Phrases." Bobby pulled the tool's trigger so we could hear the sound of the drill. "These phrases will help you concentrate on one step at a time so you can focus on the process, not the outcome.

"I'll give you one example of a power phrase I used back in the day. Repeat after me, 'Don't Quit, Can't Fail.'"

"Don't Quit, Can't Fail," we all said confidently.

Bobby had us repeat it back to him at least a half dozen times.

"You will have two minutes to come up with a Power Through Phrase of your own. This phrase, when repeated to yourself, will turn down the negative voice and turn up the positive voice. Jot this strategy down, **talk to yourself, don't listen to yourself.**"

We all started to write in our manuals. Bobby called on me to share my power through phrase in front of everybody.

"Prove Them Wrong... Prove Me Right," I said calmly.

"Not bad," said Bobby. "This time, I want you to say it like you mean it with big body language, a strong voice, and your eyes up!"

I sat up, took a deep breath and said PROVE THEM WRONG... PROVE ME RIGHT! This time I brought the juice!

Bobby said, "That's the fire we're looking for. Now, let's take it to the field. As I said, today's workout is a competition between boat crews using the sleds and the stadium stairs."

It was an intense relay race where two people would push the sled from one side of the field to the other, run up and down the stadium stairs, and then push the sled back to the sideline where they started.

My group started strong, but we couldn't keep up the pace we set and ended up finishing third. On top of losing to Kinger's boat crew, my body felt awful. My legs wouldn't stop shaking. I felt like I was going to be sick. We had gone all out trying to win the competition, but it just wasn't enough. As I sat on the turf trying to catch my breath, I missed another opportunity to talk to Faith. She walked by and looked like she could easily do the race again. We made eye contact. She smiled, but I could hardly keep my head up.

CHAPTER 42
PUSH THE ROCK

The leadership training from 5:30 to 6:00 on Wednesday was about understanding different personality styles. We took a personality survey, which was interesting and helped me understand why I worked well with some people but struggled to connect with others.

Our speaker was Mrs. Nolan, a history teacher at the school, who loved Greek mythology. Her class was incredibly challenging. She was tough and held a firm standard, but we respected her for it because she also held herself to a high standard.

She was an ultra-runner. A few times a year she competed in one hundred mile races. Despite barely being able to move, she would show up on Monday, ready to teach history.

"Frogs, I've been watching your summer workouts during my morning runs. I have to say, the new energy this year is very impressive," Mrs. Nolan said. "I'm honored to be with you today and to share one of my favorite stories that has helped me during some of my deepest and darkest times in competition. It's a story about a statue that many of you have seen in my classroom. A classic myth about a mortal named Sisyphus.

One day, Sisyphus was wandering around and came upon a meeting of the gods. He quickly hid behind a corner and listened in to the gods' conversation about the secrets of success and the meaning of life. Sisyphus then proceeded back to his normal daily routines. Now that he knew the meaning of life, he was crushing it!

"But then, he made a mistake. Sisyphus started to share with everyone in the town what he had learned from eavesdropping on the god's private conversation. Eventually, the god's found out and decided to punish him.

"The first god said, 'Let's just kill him and be done with it.' The second god said, 'Let's throw him in a cellar!' The third god said, 'No, those things are too easy. We need something better.' The fourth god said, 'I've got it! Let's make him push a rock up a hill for eternity!' The three other gods cheered and said, 'That's brilliant!'

"The fourth god added, 'And every time he pushes the rock to the top of the hill, we will shove it back down. Every time he thinks he's reached the finish line, the rock will fall back down the mountain and he'll live in a perpetual state of frustration, anger, and stress.'

"So, that's just what they did. They put him at the bottom of the mountain and sentenced him to push the rock to the top.

"For the first attempt, Sisyphus put his right shoulder into the rock. He pushed and pushed and finally made it to the top, only to have it pushed

and roll all the way back down.

"The second time up, Sisyphus put his left shoulder into the rock. By the time he got halfway up, the chafing and the rubbing was so bad, he started to bleed. Nonetheless, he made it to the top. Once again, a god shoved it and watched it roll all the way back down.

"The third time up, Sisyphus walked up the mountain backward with the rock seeming to lead the way. He used everything he had, and by the time he got to the top, he was physically and emotionally drained. This time, all the gods pushed the rock and laughed as it tumbled all the way back down.

"He started to get frustrated and angry, just as the gods were hoping to see.

"The fourth time up, Sisyphus knew there was no way he was going to make it all the way to the top—he was too exhausted. So, he got curious instead of furious and simplified his plan. Maybe he couldn't make it to the top, but if he just made it to the next tree, the next patch of dirt, the next patch of grass, then he'd eventually get to the top.

"The tree came and went. The dirt patch came and went. The patch of grass came and went. He had no energy left. He thought to himself, *Just take one more step.*

"And BOOM! That's when everything changed. All of a sudden, a switch flipped in his head. His goal was no longer to push the rock to the top of the mountain. His goal was to take one more step.

"He then became infatuated with the process. He got so excited every time he took one more step, and his momentum and energy made the step after that just a little bit easier.

"This time, when he got to the top of the mountain, he was so eager to get after it again that he shoved the rock down the mountain and chased after it with a smile on his face. He couldn't wait to get back to pushing the rock.

"See, Sisyphus stumbled upon quite possibly the greatest secret of all time. Success is hidden in the process. Don't be condemned to a life of frustration. Instead, focus on taking life one step at a time, doing what you can do without focusing on the end result. That's how we, like Sisyphus, learn.

"It's easy to fall in love with the outcome like completing a workout or celebrating a victory. Anyone can do that. But falling in love with the process, like pushing the sled, is where the major breakthroughs will happen for you. Let's take wisdom from Sisyphus and focus on the moment not the mountain.

"I know you have a success checklist through HabitShare on your phone. Initially, I was going to ask you to enter 'Push the Rock.' Based on what I've seen from this summer's training, let's enter 'Push the Sled.' I know it's subjective, as you won't be physically pushing a sled every day, so this may be harder to evaluate. **Pushing the sled is a way of life. It's about constantly putting one foot in front of the other and moving forward. It's knowing at the end of the day when your head hits the pillow, you did everything you could to attack the gap between where you are now and where you want to be.**"

We all typed "Push the Sled" into our success checklist. Then we went out to the field for another sled workout series led by Bobby. The humidity of a hot July day in Minnesota was already in the air. Even though it was only 7:30 in the morning, it was stifling hot. It felt even hotter when we got on the turf.

There was a point during the hundred-yard sled workout where I wanted to give up. My legs were fried, my t-shirt was drenched, and my mouth was as dry as a desert. I was at the thirty-five-yard line when I stopped pushing my sled. With sixty-five yards remaining in front of me, I looked over to Bobby, wishing he would blow the whistle to end the workout. Suddenly, I was Sisyphus! I needed to stop looking at the end zone or hoping Bobby would blow the whistle. Instead, I decided to talk to myself instead of listening to myself. *Take one step at a time* echoed in my head. I took a deep breath, put my head down, extended my arms, and pushed the sled. As I started to move it, my "LBL" wristband was staring at me. "Little by Little, a Little Becomes a Lot."

The next thing I knew, the hash marks on the field went by quicker. When I crossed the fifty-yard line, I smiled and worked my way into the end zone. I was proud of the fact that I stayed focused, present, and gave a high level effort even when I wanted to quit.

At the end of the workout, Bobby thanked Mrs. Nolan for her message of Sisyphus and for jumping into the workout to push the sled with us.

"It was my pleasure!" she said as she wiped the sweat from her forehead. She then reached into her duffle bag and pulled out a miniature stone sculpture of Sisyphus.

"I'd like to give this sculpture to Leah, who worked exceptionally hard today. I know she has dreams of swimming at the college level. Leah, if you continue to work like you did today when you are in the pool, I have no doubt your dream will come true."

We all clapped loudly as a surprised Leah stood up to accept the Sisyphus replica.

CHAPTER 43
THE REST OF WEEK THREE

After the workout on Thursday, I finally found the courage to talk to Faith. We talked about the summer program and her job at the waterpark. I asked her what she was doing for the rest of the day, secretly hoping she planned to come back for the Champions Do More workout that afternoon.

She said the entire Daxter family was headed up north to their cabin for the week. This bummed me out.

"But," she smiled and said, "I will see you back here on the Monday after the fourth."

She had a way about her that was unlike any other girl I'd ever met. I was glad that I had an actual conversation with her and could finally check that off on my HabitShare app.

Later that day, Kinger stopped by the house to pick up Olivia.

"What's up, Action?" Kinger asked. Without waiting for my response, he added, "I'm taking Liv to the beach. You want to roll with us?"

It bugged me that Kinger was taking my sister to the beach. I just didn't like the guy. Plus, if they are going to the beach, it meant they wouldn't be at the Champions Do More workout, again.

"No, I'm going back to the school to push the sled," I said.

"Bruh, you sure are drinking the Kool-Aid," Kinger said with a laugh.

"He sure is," said Liv as she walked up to the car. "He's like the poster child... the frog man, I mean... for Whitlock, and the teacher's pet for Bobsled Bobby." She snickered.

"Well, keep doing that share your habit deal and pushing that rock, champ. We need someone who can complete a pass this season. I can't do it all myself again." Kinger's tone had an unmistakable hint of sarcasm as he and my sister sped off to the beach.

CHAPTER 44
THE WEEK OF JULY 4TH

Despite not setting the alarm on my phone, I woke up at my usual time of 5:20 on Monday morning. I guess the power of habit Bobby was talking about was legit. Plus, the training was paying off. I could see the results in the mirror. I felt stronger than ever and I didn't want to lose momentum by doing nothing for a week. As I flipped through our manual looking for a sled workout, I came across Dax's quote, "The things that are easy to do are easy not to do." After I clicked "complete" on all my morning checklist items on HabitShare, I headed to the field.

I thought I would be the only one there since it was our week off. However, I wasn't the only person who woke up early. Bobby Bobsled was already on the field, pushing a sled and getting after it.

"Action, I didn't expect to see you this morning. How's it going?" Bobby asked as sweat dripped from his forehead.

"Ahh... It's going okay."

"Sounds like you're not okay. What's on your mind?"

"Nothing big, I guess. It's just that I used to look forward to the week of July fourth as a kid. Our family would always rent a huge cabin up north. My cousins on both sides of the family would join us for a few days. It was a blast. We grilled, swam, tubed, and lit off fireworks into the lake. After my parents split up, the days of renting a cabin ended."

"That's rough. It sounds like those were some good times," said Bobby.

"They were great times. Just kinda hit me hard today," I said.

I was surprised that he didn't offer me cheap advice by saying something like, "It could be worse." Instead, he stayed curious, listened, and asked questions without any judgment.

"What else is on your mind?" asked Bobby.

"I don't know. I always wanted to be a leader. It's cool the team voted me captain. It's just tougher than I thought."

Bobby nodded. "Very true, Jackson. What's the real challenge for you here?"

"Well, I just get sick and tired of a few people's negative comments about working hard. Sometimes when I challenge my boat crew, I catch them rolling their eyes. Last week, I overheard a teammate imitate me as a boat crew leader. When I asked him about it, he said, 'Relax, man, I'm just kidding. Can't you take a joke?' Even my own sister makes fun of me for working hard. If it's like that this summer, what's it going to be like during the school year?"

CHAPTER 45
LIKED VERSUS LIKABLE

"What do you really want?" asked Bobby in a calm and caring voice.

It took me a minute. "I want to be liked by my teammates. I want them to respect me when I call them up. And I want them to work hard like I do."

"Seems like you're frustrated. How can I help?" asked Bobby.

"Put my family back together and have everyone like me and respect what I say."

Both of us laughed at this unrealistic thought.

"Well, I can't help you with the family piece. But let's chat about the 'being liked' part. Let me ask you another question. What qualities come to mind when you think of a person who is likeable?"

"They're friendly, sincere, good at listening, caring, and they have a sense of humor," I said.

"Nice. We could probably add humble, kind, and respectful, I imagine," Bobby added. "Jackson, could you be all of those things we just listed and still not be liked by a few people?"

I found myself staring at Bobby. "I suppose that's true."

"No matter what you do, somebody is not going to like it. Say you're working on a group project and you decide to just stay quiet. Even if you never said a single word, someone would be upset because you never shared your ideas.

"Control what you can control," Bobby said. "The reality is, we're all going to be judged by others. You have some *influence* on how others see and judge you. But at the end of the day, you simply can't *control* how they will see or judge you. I've learned this lesson the hard way."

"So, if we are going to be judged by others, does it make sense to be as likeable as possible, do what you think is right, and then let the chips fall where they may?" Bobby asked.

"I never thought of it like that. I guess I need to keep pushing myself and others while being okay knowing some people aren't going to like it. Even if some of those people are in my own family.

"I feel like a weight has been lifted off my shoulders."

"Good. Now, let's take some of that weight, put it on the sled, and get to work," said Bobby.

"Yeah! Let's do that."

As we started walking toward the sled, a few other athletes showed up. Bobby welcomed them and pulled out a few more sleds. It was a routine we followed for the next four days.

Thursday was the fourth of July, and Bobby put together a special sled workout for us.

"Hard to believe we're already halfway through the summer, Frogs. I'm proud of each of you for showing up on your week off. Let's stay fired up!" he said, as he lit the sparklers that were taped to the sleds. He blasted Lee Greenwood's "Proud to Be an American" over the sound system. "I'm proud to be an American and I'm proud of all you who showed up this week. Last rep for today. Let's make it a down and back for a last two hundred-yard push. Then go enjoy the rest of the day."

As I walked off the turf, I started to think about Monday. I was excited to see Faith again but wondered if the attendance at summer training would drop off dramatically like it had in the past.

1. Stanier, Michael Bungay. "Say Less, Ask More & Change the Way You Lead Forever" *The Mindset Advantage podcast, iTunes app. February 2023*

CHAPTER 46
TACTICAL SKILL #4 – SELF-CONTROL AND DISCIPLINE

"Frogs, CHECK IN!"

Our "all in" response wasn't impressive. This wasn't much of a surprise given that most of the others had been off for an entire week.

"Ouch, that was brutal," Whitlock said with a disgusted look on her face.

The energy in the auditorium was much lower than before. Looking around, I saw that we were probably missing twenty athletes. Not bad, considering we usually lost half the group after July 4th.

"Let's try that again. CHECK IN!"

"ALL IN!" we shouted back.

Kinger was sitting next to Faith and seemed to be flirting with her. Not only was he taking my sister to the beach, but he was also now talking to the girl I was interested in getting to know better. He was getting on my nerves and was probably just trying to get under my skin. It was working... big time.

"Well, here we are in week four, almost halfway through summer training. Do you realize we are closer to the first day of school than the last day of school?" asked Whitlock.

"That sucks," I heard Kinger say soft enough so Whitlock didn't hear it.

"This week, we will uncover Tactical Skill #4, which is Self-Control and Discipline. Take a look at your manual. Before we can gain self-control and discipline, we need to examine the following principles."

"Now, pick out the one that resonates with you the most and circle it."

I circled number two because even though I had very little control over what Kinger or Olivia did or said, I did have total control over how I chose to respond.

SELF CONTROL & DISCIPLINE

1. You have to be in control of yourself before you can control your performance.

2. You have very little control over what goes on around you, but you have total control over how you choose to respond to it.

3. Discipline = Freedom

4. Discipline yourself so nobody else needs to.

5. Your discipline determines your destiny.

CHAPTER 47
DRILL #7 – MAKE YOUR BED

"Question for you," Coach Whitlock said. "How many of you made your bed this morning?"

Only a handful of hands went up, and mine was not one of them.

Coach Whitlock went on, "To some, this drill appears boring and unrelated to performance. Let me drop some wisdom, **boring inputs lead to exciting outputs**. Making your bed every morning helps you develop self-control and discipline. I started doing this when I was on Team USA, and the effect it had on me was profound. The simple task of making my bed every day taught me three lessons, which are on this slide."

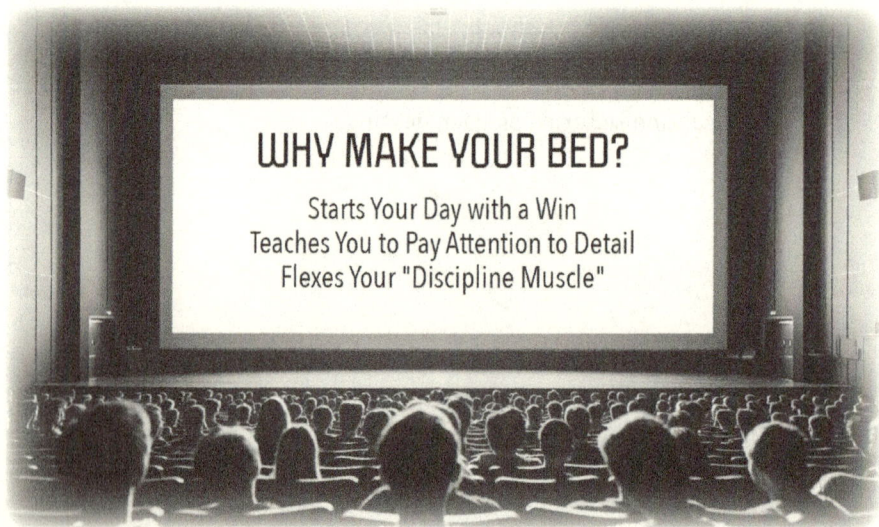

WHY MAKE YOUR BED?
Starts Your Day with a Win
Teaches You to Pay Attention to Detail
Flexes Your "Discipline Muscle"

"One, I never *feel* like making my bed. But when I do it anyway, I start the day with a win. It reminds me that I am in control of what I do. You can feel tired and lazy and still work out. Most of you probably agree that sometimes the hardest part of our workouts is just getting here in the morning. Once you start moving, you start acting different than how you felt. Let's not wait for the feel to be ideal.

"My dad used to always tell me that **champions live on the other side of 'I don't feel like it.'**

"Two. Making your bed every morning is a sign that you pay attention to detail, and you are not sloppy. Plus, I just sleep better when I get in a bed that's made. How many of you know what I'm talking about?"

Almost everyone nodded.

"Finally, we grow the muscle of discipline by doing the little things we promised ourselves we would do.

"So, here's your challenge. For the rest of the week, set your alarm one minute earlier than normal. When you wake up, make your bed. Start the day with a win, pay attention to detail, flex your mental muscles, and become a person who has self-control and discipline. If this is new for you, watch the shock on the faces of those who are raising you. They will probably wonder if you are alright," Whitlock joked.

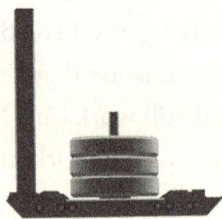

CHAPTER 48

DRILL #8 – RELEASE ROUTINE

"I have another question for you," Coach Whitlock said. "How many of you have made a mistake in a game, competition, or contest and let it spiral into a series of poor decisions and bad plays?"

This time, hands slowly went into the air.

"We are all going to make mistakes and bad plays from time to time," Whitlock said with a smile.

"One of the major differences between elite athletes and average athletes is the speed in which they can refocus after facing the inevitable obstacles that come with playing sports. The second drill for today will help prevent you from spiraling into an endless stream of bad plays," Whitlock said confidently.

"Your personal release routine is made up of a three-step process. As you know, **in order to trust the process, you first need to have a process**. Go to drill #8 in your manual."

"The first step in your release routine is a physical action that signifies you are letting go and moving forward. This could be wiping your jersey, clapping your hands, re-strapping your gloves, grabbing and throwing the dirt, the list goes on. What you choose for your physical action doesn't have to be flashy, but it needs to resonate with you.

"The second step is to take a deep breath and look at a focal point.

This is often the most overlooked step in the release routine. Taking a deep breath with a long inhale and a longer exhale helps to regulate your nervous system, brings you back to the present moment, and gives clarity in chaotic moments. While performing your long breath, I want you to find a focal point that you know will be at every stadium, field, gymnasium, or whatever platform that you compete in. This could be a flagpole, the press box, the shot clock, or the top of the fence. Ideally this focal point sits above your eye level so when you lock into it, your head will be held high, and you will automatically be demonstrating confident body language.

"The third and final step is to use one of your power phrases you created last Monday.

"Ideally, the three-step process is used sequentially. Now, depending on your sport and the situation, you may need to adjust your release routine. For example, as a hockey player, your release routine will be different during a line change versus when you make a poor pass. While each sport is different, the three-step process is universal."

After we created our personalized release routine, Coach Whitlock had us close our eyes and visualize an in-game mistake followed by our release routine. Next, we all stood up in the auditorium and rehearsed our new release routine.

I loved this drill, and I couldn't wait to use it in the fall!

Scan the QR Code to watch a video of a release routine by Brian Cain

CHAPTER 49
CHANCE FAVORS THE PREPARED

At the 5:30 a.m. leadership training, Coach Whitlock focused on pre-season questions that should be discussed with our coaches before the season started. Whitlock noted the questions were taken from the book *High School Sports Leader*. I wrote them in my manual:

PRE-SEASON ATHLETE TO COACH QUESTIONS

1. What do you expect from me this season?

2. When there is a problem or issue, what's our process to address it?

3. What do I need to know that I don't know now?

I planned to schedule a time with Coach Allen to go through each question.

This week's Winning Edge Wednesday's guest speaker was going to be on Zoom. Whitlock had hyped up this "major league" guest since Monday.

I was dying to find out who it was. Moments later, major league baseball player, three-time All Star, and World Series champ Matt Carpenter appeared on the screen. Yankee Stadium was visible from his hotel window.

I couldn't believe Coach Whitlock got one of my favorite baseball players of all time to speak to us!

"Hey Frogs, it's good to be with you bright and early this morning. When Coach Whitlock called and shared the Separation Through Preparation training with me, I was very impressed," Carpenter said. "I only wish I had received this vital combination of physical and mental training when I was your age. You are lucky to have Coach Whitlock running the show. When she told me Bobby Bobsled was joining her, I was seriously jealous. It wasn't until I made it to the big leagues that I was introduced to some of the same mental drills and skills you are getting now in high school. In the majors, we all do physical drills like hitting and fielding every day. I've also added daily mental drills to improve my game. My favorite drills are concentration grids for pre-game focus, well-better-how for post-game reflection, and of course HabitShare for tracking my consistency with the things that matter to me most. As a professional baseball player, if I don't work those drills consistently, I know my time at this level will get cut short, and I want to be here for as long as possible. As I look back on my career, one simple yet profound lesson has absolutely changed my life." Carpenter paused and cleared his throat, "**Chance favors the prepared and preparation means being there before you get there.**"

I looked around the room and noticed everyone's eyes on the screen. This seemed to be the most *into it* the whole group had been all summer.

Matt went on, "'I will prepare, and someday my chance will come.' That quote from Abraham Lincoln is painted on the wall of my home gym. Notice that the quote starts with *prepare*. It doesn't say 'I will hope and someday my chance will come.' No, it says *I will prepare*. Hope is a start, but it's not enough. If you have a big final exam in front of you, hope can't be your top strategy to do well. When you're prepared, you have a better chance of knocking it out of the park!"

CHAPTER 50
PRE-GAME YOUR PRE-GAME

"People often ask me how I get ready for a game. The answer is, I pre-game my pre-game. I have a very specific routine that I follow when I get to the field. I do it for each practice and for all one hundred and sixty-two games we play in a season. My pre-game routine helps me flip the switch mentally from being a dad to being a baseball player. For you, it's like flipping the switch from student to athlete. It's getting ready to get ready, so you get the most out of that day's work. I also have a prepared release routine that helps me get back into the zone when I find myself swinging at bad pitches or making errors in the field. It sounds like you went through release routines on Monday. I sure could have used that as a young baseball player. My release routine after a called strike three was to throw my bat in the dugout. After a fielding error, I would cuss like a sailor. I found myself reacting instead of responding. What I didn't understand was that my reaction was not only bad for me but it also impacted my teammates negatively. Not good. Please learn from my foolishness. Visualization is another big part of my routine. I know Coach Whitlock and Coach Bobby will continue to give you strategies on visualization. Make sure you use them."

Carpenter leaned into his screen, lowered his voice, and said, "Chance favors the prepared. How well are you preparing this summer? Are you working your butt off and taking all the physical and mental drills and skills seriously? Or are you sitting back, crossing your fingers, and hoping it works out for the best? Maybe you're in a reserve role right now. Good. More time to prepare. Hey, you never know when something out of the ordinary will happen and your name gets called. How sad would it be to have your chance, the opportunity you've worked for and dreamed suddenly appear, but YOU WEREN'T PREPARED?" Carpenter shook his head in disgust. That, my Pine Lake friends, would be brutal."

"Once your season gets going, will you prepare for practice or just wait for practice?

"Prepare, and your chance will come."

Carpenter was getting me fired up! I still couldn't believe *the* Matt Carpenter was talking to us. Unreal.

"**You only get one chance to be a high school athlete.** Seniors, please stand up."

Without hesitation, I stood with the rest of the seniors.

"Twelve short months from now, many of you will be packing up and heading off to a whole new life. Are you prepared to quit making excuses and start executing? Will you look back at your high school athletic and academic career with pride, knowing you went all out? What about socially? Is there someone you want to ask out but you are too afraid of them saying no? Hey, what if they said yes? Will you look back at your senior year with regret, knowing you were more of a holdout than an all-out? You decide, I have a feeling it's going to be a big year at Pine Lake!

"Frogs! Chance favors the prepared!"

The rest of the audience stood up and applauded as Matt Carpenter waved goodbye.

Coach Whitlock took the mic. "I told you that was going to be a major league message. Let's take this enthusiasm into our workout and crush some sled jacks. Let's go, Frogs!"

CHAPTER 51
END OF WEEK 4

Thursday night at the dinner table, my mom asked Olivia and me what we learned this week.

"Not much. Just another week of training," Olivia said. "We had some baseball guy talk to us on Zoom. He was pretty good, I guess."

"She's talking about Matt Carpenter, one of the best players in the major leagues," I said.

"He talked about how chance favors the prepared and to remember that we only have one chance to be a high school athlete, so we need to make the most of it by going all out."

"Good stuff," said my mom. "Growing up, my dad always told me, **'You can make excuses, or you can make it happen.'**"

"Sounds like Grandpa would have liked Coach Whitlock," I added.

Much to my surprise, Olivia added, "I guess there was actually something that I might be able to use. You guys know I get so frustrated when I double fault. So, I hope my release routine will keep me from freaking out and double faulting again."

"Release routine?" my mom asked.

"Basically, it's a three-step process to help me move forward and get back in the zone when I mess up. Here, I'll show you." She grabbed her tennis racquet that was leaning against the chair where my dad used to sit.

"When I double fault, I'm going to wipe my jersey with my right hand. That's my physical action. Then, I'm going to hold my racquet out in front of me, take a deep breath in and out while I look at the strings in the center. Then I say my 'Power Phrase,' which is, 'new serve, new chance.'"

I smiled. "You mean you were actually paying attention, Olivia?"

Olivia looked at me and did her famous eye roll. "Jackson, you're such a jerk."

Mom chimed in, "Hey, that's pretty cool, Olivia. I can't wait to see that at your next match! Guess what? I have a new release routine, too. I snap my fingers and you both start clearing the table." She laughed at her own joke.

CHAPTER 52
TACTICAL SKILL #5 – VISUALIZATION

We walked into the auditorium for Mental Performance Monday to a video playing. We watched athletes in a variety of sports doing what looked like some sort of meditation and pretending to play their sport.

"CHECK IN!" Coach Whitlock said into the mic as the clock hit exactly 6:00.

"ALL IN!" we echoed back.

"Let's get right to it. We have a lot to do today. This week, we uncover what many top coaches and athletes call 'the missing link' in all of sports and performance. You heard Matt Carpenter mention it last week. I'm talking about Tactical Skill #5, Visualization," Coach Whitlock said.

"Real quick, turn to the person next to you and give them directions to your house from the school."

I turned around because the person on my left and on my right were already in conversation. Boom, who was right behind me? Faith Daxter.

As I stumbled with my words to give her directions to my house, she laughed and then gave me directions to her house with ease. It turned out she lived a few neighborhoods away from me. I had no idea.

"By a show of hands, how many of you actually visualized the route in your mind as you gave directions?" Coach Whitlock asked.

We all smiled and raised our hands.

"Of course, you did. It's almost impossible not to. I also noticed a lot of you closed your eyes. That helped you to see the roads and the turns as you were explaining the route to your partner. All of you just experienced visualization.

Let's not confuse daydreaming with visualization. Daydreaming is just letting your thoughts wander with no guidance or purpose. Visualization is being intentional and purposeful with your thoughts.

As Whitlock picked out a manual that had the Olympic logo on it she continued, "This is pretty high level stuff, but I want to share with you a powerful study revolving around a term called functional equivalence.

Whitlock opened the manual and continued, "Basically, the research on functional equivalence has proven that your brain has the remarkable ability to strengthen the neural pathways used when performing specific motor skills simply through the act of mental practice.

Turns out, when you visualize a specific action, your brain records it in the same way as it would have if you were actually doing it and treats the imagined practice or situation as if it was real.

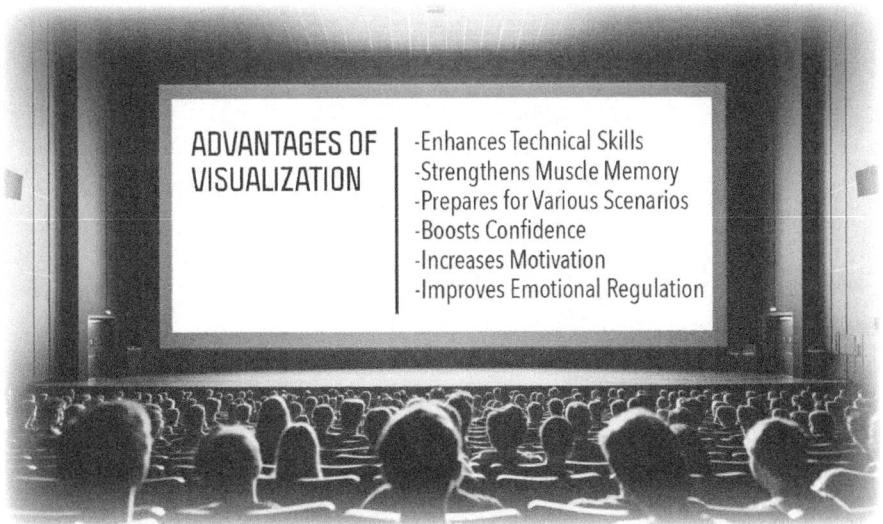

ADVANTAGES OF VISUALIZATION
- Enhances Technical Skills
- Strengthens Muscle Memory
- Prepares for Various Scenarios
- Boosts Confidence
- Increases Motivation
- Improves Emotional Regulation

If you've ever watched a scary scene in a movie and felt your heart rate jump, you just experienced functional equivalence.

"Here's the really exciting part," Whitlock continued. "By going over the steps, techniques, and various situations in your mind, you can refine your skills without physical strain and allow for repetition and adjustments. This works for visualizing how you want it to go, how it could go, and how to respond when adversity strikes.

The amazing thing is over time, by executing these visualized moments, they start to become automatic during a game or contest.

This must have been why Bobby emphasized why I needed to stop obsessing on the interception and start visualizing all the other plays that went well.

1. A.J. Adams, MAPP (Masters in Applied Positive Psychology)

CHAPTER 53
DRILL #9 - SHADOW WORK

"There are two drills I want to share with you today about visualization. The first is an active drill called shadow work. It's what you saw on the screen when you walked in today," Coach Whitlock explained.

"Shadow Work is where you combine the physical and mental side of your sport without equipment like a ball, stick, bat, baton, etc. One advantage of shadow work is that it can be done almost anywhere provided you have space to actively move around.

"Here's how it works. You pick an aspect of your sport you want to focus on. Depending on your sport, you may work on cadence, timing, rhythm, footwork, or routines. Just like actors do dress rehearsals without an audience, top-notch athletes take the same approach.

"Remove the outcome. It's not about the scoreboard for this drill. This will allow you to fully immerse yourself into the process.

"Check out the screen. Here are five areas you can develop through Shadow Work:

"Hit the QR CODE at the bottom of the screen to see it in action.

"I wasn't even aware of Shadow Work until I got to the Olympic level. Some people don't try it because they think they will look stupid practicing without their equipment.

"Maybe you've heard me say this a few times already this summer.

I'm telling you—it will work..." she opened her palm to us.

"When you work it," we responded back without hesitation.

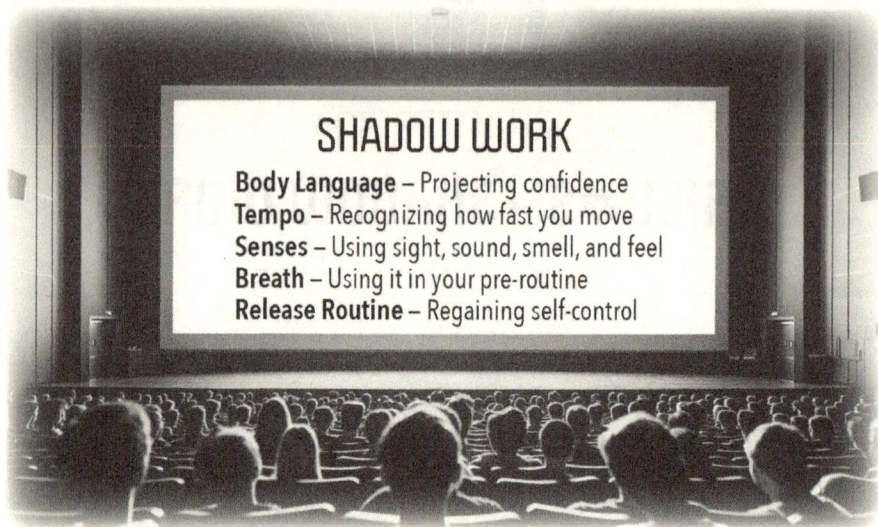

SHADOW WORK
Body Language – Projecting confidence
Tempo – Recognizing how fast you move
Senses – Using sight, sound, smell, and feel
Breath – Using it in your pre-routine
Release Routine – Regaining self-control

Scan the QR Code to watch
Video Examples of Shadow Reps from
Brian Cain

CHAPTER 54
DRILL #10 – GET ON THE BALL

"The second drill of the day is called BALL visualization. While shadow work is *active*. The BALL drill is *passive*. In other words, you don't have to physically move to use the drill. Let's fill in the blanks for ball framework on page twelve."

Whitlock then put up another QR code that took us to a YouTube playlist of sport-specific visualization videos we could do on our own. She clicked the first video and asked us all to close our eyes.

At first it was kind of weird. *Was this really going to help me perform better on Friday nights?* I wondered.

During the video, we were asked to visualize a previous best performance. Something clicked. For the first time since I threw the game ending interception, I was able to recall other successful plays from that last game. Seeing those positive moments of coming off the bench and playing well actually gave me some confidence. Up to that point, despite Bobby's advice, I had only visualized the interception.

I liked the visualization drill, and it was something I could easily add to my pre-game routine.

Coach Whitlock then asked us to add Drill #8 Shadow Work and #9 BALL Visualization to our success checklist on HabitShare.

We went out to the field and got into our sport-specific groups. It was a bit comical seeing all of us pretend to play our sports with no equipment.

While it was awkward at first to practice taking a shotgun snap and rolling right for a pretend pass without a football in my hand, I could see how this drill might work.

Of course, there would always be people like Kinger, who were too cool for school and made fun of the drill. I couldn't control the way they acted. I could only control my response.

GET ON THE BALL

B = Breathing and body scan to relax

A = Affirming through self-talk

L = Looking back at previous best performances

L = Looking forward to your next performance. See yourself competing the way you want to compete

Scan the QR Code for
A Mental Imagery Playlist

CHAPTER 55
THE ENEMY THANKS YOU

Two days later, our 5:30 leadership workshop involved a construction activity. Coach Whitlock gave each group twenty-five straws and a piece of masking tape. The goal was to build the tallest tower we could, but none of the straws could be taped to the floor. She cranked the music intentionally, which made communication difficult. It was fun and frustrating. Twice, our tower fell because the base was too narrow. One of the major lessons was that direct and clear communication is at the base of leadership.

The Winning Edge Wednesday guest speaker was our local Navy recruiter. Coach Buzz, as we all called him, was also our school's wrestling and linebacker coach. He was proud to have served three tours overseas. He also was a graduate of Pine Lake and kind of a local hero. He was at least six foot four, kept a military haircut, and was in excellent shape. He had an intimating look that could make even the toughest of the tough feel scared.

"Frogs, what an honor to serve you today. I sat in the back of the auditorium last week and watched Matt Carpenter on the big screen. How cool was that?" Buzz said.

"It wasn't that long ago when I sat in the seats you are in now. If I could tell my high school self three life lessons, this is what they would be.

"**The enemy thanks you.** That's the first lesson, and it comes from my time in the Navy."

I could see the emotion building inside of Buzz. Even though he was known to be cool, calm, and collected, he paused for maybe ten seconds. It looked like he was on the verge of shedding a tear.

"When you take a day off, the enemy thanks you. When you take shortcuts, the enemy thanks you. When you bash at the beach and your workouts suffer the next day or three, the enemy thanks you.

"Of course, in high school sports, you don't face enemies, you face opponents. The opponent doesn't thank you with their words. They thank you by beating you in competition because you didn't care enough about yourself or your teammates to prepare. Here at Pine Lake, if you get beat in a game, it sucks for a while, then life goes on. However, in combat, the stakes are higher, because lives are literally on the line.

"Sometimes you can do all the right things and still lose. That's sports. The best team doesn't always win. But the team that plays the best usually does. Let's not put ourselves in a position where our opponent thanks us."

Buzz was on a roll. I thought.

CHAPTER 56
NERVOUS AND CONFIDENT

"The second life lesson I wish I knew at your age is that **you can be nervous and confident at the same time.** It's not one or the other. I bet as an athlete there have been times when you were nervous and still performed well. I'll also wager there have been times when you were confident but performed poorly. See, I used to think being nervous before a game or a military mission was bad. It's not!"

I couldn't believe it. Here was the toughest human being I had ever met talking about being nervous. I didn't think Coach Buzz was nervous about anything.

"Being nervous can be used to your advantage. Why? Turn to page twenty in your manuals to read about the advantages of feeling nervous."

"Let's break these down," said Buzz. "The number one advantage of being nervous is it shows you care about what's in front of you. Chances are something amazing could be right around the corner.

"Number two. It fuels your preparation. Often, your best week of practice stems from being a little nervous about the next game, and your effort and focus are stronger. What can you do when you have big time nerves?

"I remember when I was with the SEALs, and we were in the cargo vans heading to a dangerous mission. My stomach was filled with butterflies, and I could tell my fellow soldiers sitting next to me were feeling the nerves as well.

"During those dark drives heading into the unknown, we would all fuel our preparation by focusing on our breathing. The strategy that helped us the most was having longer exhales than our inhales. For example, we would inhale for four seconds and exhale for eight, sometimes in unison. A performance expert on base taught us that if we did that breathing cadence for twelve cycles, we could trigger our parasympathetic nervous system otherwise known as rest and digest. This process would calm us down and help us focus on the mission in front of us.

Let's try it as a group. Coach Buzz asked us to close our eyes and he coached us through the breathing cadence.

It didn't take long for me to notice my heart rate start to slow down.

This stuff really works!

"The third advantage of being nervous is it invites you to see pressure as a privilege. There are not a lot of opportunities in life where you get to feel that pre-game pressure. Ask any former athlete what they miss about high school sports, and they will tell you they miss the feeling of standing next to their teammates, stomach turning, while the national anthem played. That's not going to happen when you go out into the workforce. Buzz chuckled, "You aren't going to line up for the national anthem at an office job, manufacturing line, or construction project.

"You *get* to be a part of high school sports. You don't *have* to be a part of high school sports. So, instead of trying to fight off the nerves, let's embrace them and use them to our advantage. Say yes if you're with me, Frogs?"

"Yes!" we shouted back.

"Whooo, man, I get fired up talking about this stuff. Before I get too caught up, stay with me. I have a third life lesson to share with you."

CHAPTER 57
CONTINGENCY PLANNING

Coach Buzz continued, "**Contingency Planning** is life lesson number three. 'Everyone has a plan until you get hit in the mouth.' That's from Mike Tyson. When you get hit with adversity and everything is going wrong, what are you going to do? How are you going to respond?

"In the Navy, we did daily contingency drills for what to do when things went wrong or got tough. We did underwater contingency drills fifty feet below the surface to help us stay calm when our scuba mask started to fill with water. This happened to me on two separate real-life missions. Both times, I relied on the contingency drills, and I recovered successfully.

"Let's look at an example outside of the Navy. Who has ever experienced a flat tire?"

Looking at Faith, Buzz asked, "Did you know you would be dealing with a flat tire that day?"

"Not at all. It happened last summer on our way to a volleyball tournament. We were going about seventy-five on Interstate 35. We were all freaked out. My dad said it was the first flat tire he'd ever had," Faith said.

"Sounds scary," said Buzz. "Contingency Planning is accepting that it's not going to be perfect and positive all the time. Sometimes you will face flat tire situations like ugly weather, a hostile away crowd, or a player's injury.

"Athletes and teams who practice contingency plans create a major

119

competitive advantage. When a flat tire scenario happens, instead of overreacting because their nerves got in the way, they reach for whatever would be equivalent to a spare tire and execute their contingency plan.

"Les Brown, the famous motivational speaker, said it best. 'It's better to be prepared for an opportunity and not have one than to have an opportunity and not be prepared.'

"Let's take shadow reps and contingency planning seriously. Let's reframe being nervous as a sign that you are prepared to compete. See it like something amazing is about to happen. See being nervous as your advantage."

The applause was loud and proud. We truly saw Coach Buzz as an American Hero. I quickly created a new note in my phone on what I learned from Coach Buzz.

The sled workout that day was the best one yet. The energy was high, the music was loud, and we were all fired up from Coach Buzz's speech. Even Olivia and Kinger were dialed in.

Coach Bobby had us doing shuttle sprints and hand-over-hand sled pulls using fifty-foot ropes. It was a grueling combo that left us with a major bicep pump.

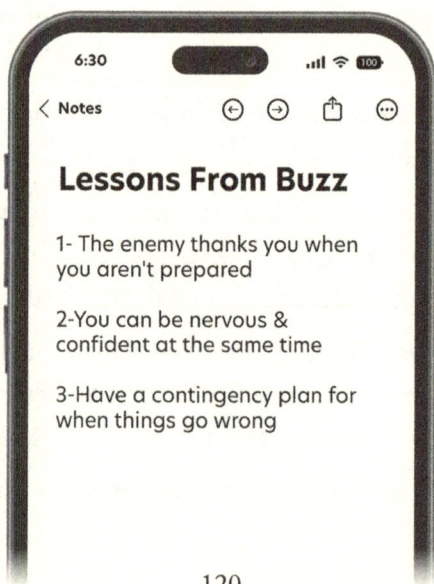

6:30 .ul 🛜 100

< Notes

Lessons From Buzz

1- The enemy thanks you when you aren't prepared

2-You can be nervous & confident at the same time

3-Have a contingency plan for when things go wrong

CHAPTER 58
END OF WEEK 5

There is something special about the number five. It's my jersey number, the month I was born, and the day I was born. So naturally, it's become my favorite number. Week five was filled with a lot of new ideas. I started to do my shadow work and BALL visualizations. My biggest takeaway was that I could be nervous and confident at the same time. It wasn't one or the other.

I also had another real conversation with Faith after one of the Champions Do More workouts. She was so mature for a sixteen-year-old. I had Matt Carpenter's voice in the back of my head reminding me not to have any regrets. I found myself just wanting to be around her more. I even parked my car in the area where she normally parked her Jeep, hoping to walk out of the workout together in the same direction.

WHO AM I?

I am your constant companion.

I am your greatest helper or heaviest burden.

I will push you onward or drag you down to failure.

I am completely at your command.

Half of the things you do might as well be turned over to me and I will do them—quickly and correctly.

Show me exactly how you want something done, and after a few lessons, I will do it automatically.

Those who are great, I have made great.

Those who are failures, I have made failures.

I am not a machine, although I work with the precision of a machine plus the intelligence of a person.

Train me, and I will place the world at your feet.

Be easy with me and I will destroy you.

Who am I?

CHAPTER 59
TACTICAL SKILL #6 – ROUTINES AND HABITS OF EXCELLENCE

As we walked into the auditorium for Mental Performance Monday for week six, the coaches handed us a page for our manual that had riddle on it.

Coach Whitlock asked. "What's the answer to the riddle??"

After some time, Olivia raised her hand and shouted, "Habit... I am Habit." Olivia was always good at solving riddles.

"That's right!" Coach Whitlock said. "The secrets of your success are hidden in your daily routines and habits. Almost every result you get is a lagging measure of your habits that proceed them. Your physical fitness is a lagging measure of your training habits. Your grades in school are a lagging measure of your study habits. Even the small stuff like the clutter in your locker is a lagging measure of your cleaning habits. **We don't rise to the level of our goals, we sink to the level of our habits.** So, if you want to see a change in your outputs, you need to fix your inputs.

"James Clear, author of Atomic Habits says, "Every action you take is a vote for the type of person you wish to become.

"The question that begs to be asked is, 'Are your votes bringing you closer or further away from the type of person you are hoping to become?'"

I felt the entire room nodding back at Whitlock.

"Look, if you master your habits, it doesn't necessarily guarantee results, but it's hard to find something that puts you in a better position to get great results."

Whitlock paused for a moment to let that thought sink in.

"Let's get after it today, shall we?" Whitlock asked.

"I thought we had already been getting after it," chirped Kinger, clearly reaching for a cheap laugh but without getting one.

It felt like people were getting tired of his comments and poor attitude. I doubt that would stop him, though.

CHAPTER 60
DRILL #11 – START-STOP-CONTINUE

"It doesn't matter your sport, your age, or your ability level. If want to become the best version of yourself, you must master these four factors of personal health," Whitlock said with passion as she put up the next slide.

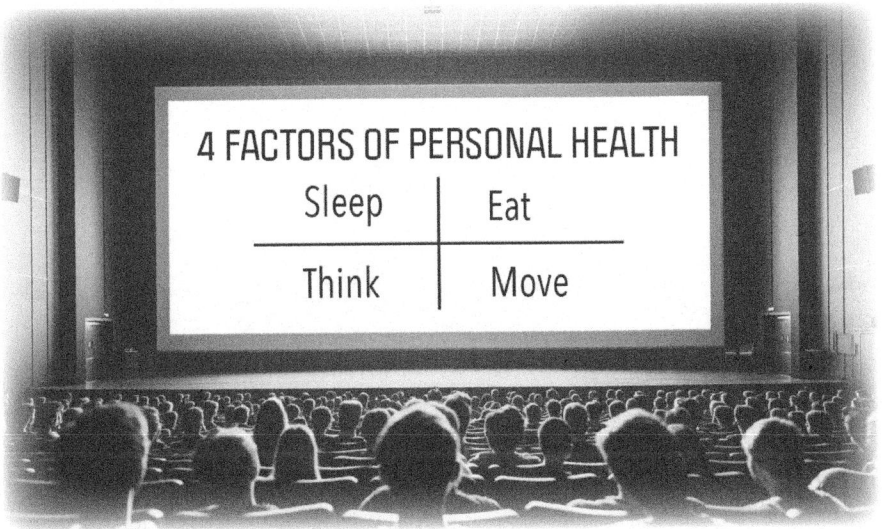

"Taking the time to examine and then optimize your routines and habits will give you the best chance for success. To do this, we will use drill # 11, Start–Stop–Continue with each factor of the STEM framework.

"Here's my personal Start–Stop–Continue for July."

The boat captains handed out Whitlock's form that we added to our manuals.

"Please open your manuals to the STEM page. Let's spread out and take ten minutes to complete drill #11 on your own."

Who knew Coach Whitlock and I both loved TikTok? As tough as it was going to be, I also wrote down "Stop scrolling TikTok after thirty minutes. More goal, less scroll." I'm going to limit myself to thirty minutes because I can usually spend well over an hour mindlessly scrolling when I should be sleeping. I knew that would be a major change for me.

START-STOP-CONTINUE

SLEEP

Start: Getting into bed at 9:00
Stop: Having my phone next to the bed
Continue: Shutting off screens at 8:30

THINK

Start: Journaling at the end of every day
Stop: Scrolling TikTok for more than 20 minutes
Continue: Listening to:
The Mindset Advantage with DJ Hillier
Mental Performance Daily with Brian Cain
Increase Your Impact with Justin Su'a

EAT

Start: Drinking 2/3 of body weight in ounces of water daily
Stop: Drinking more than one energy drink per day
Continue: Eating the same number of grams of protein as my body weight in pounds

MOVE

Start: Implementing a ten-minute mobility routine
Stop: Sitting at the desk while planning and writing
Continue: Going on daily walks around Pine Lake with my father

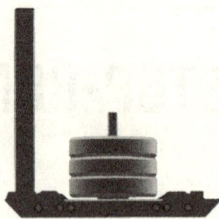

CHAPTER 61
GAINING TRUST

Wednesday's 5:30 a.m. leadership training with Coach Whitlock focused on execution. We divided into groups of four and built a ship using Legos. Each person was given an envelope with a specific set of instructions for a part of the ship. Once everyone completed their part, we just needed to put it together. Because some people didn't do their part and follow directions, what should have taken a few minutes took twenty instead. It was frustrating!

In our debrief, Coach Whitlock leaned on some Dax humor. "Did you see what can happen when you are trying to build a leader*SHIP* and some people don't follow directions? The leader*SHIP* sinks!" She laughed at her own play on words.

"Leaders must communicate, give, and follow directions, then execute the plan in order to get results. Consistent results build trust. It's going to be hard for people to follow you and do their job if they don't trust you," Coach Whitlock said.

"Here's the goal for today. When we get to the field after today's speaker, I want to have all the boat crews complete a synchronized series of five burpees, ten sit-ups, fifteen squats, and one set of Sled Jacks using the FROGS cadence. That means when all the boat crews have successfully completed the task, you are done for the day.

"Here's a new twist on our integrity standard. We will go through all four exercises without stopping and then do a large group integrity check. If you or anyone else had a mess up, but you owned it and called yourself on it, we start a new series. However, you will add one repetition to each exercise. This means Tactical Skill #2, Focus and Awareness, will come into play because you need to be focused on the correct number of reps and aware of your timing as a boat crew.

"The coaches will serve as referees. If we notice an athlete mess up and they don't own the mistake during our integrity check, two reps will be added to each exercise.

"Oh geez, it's already 5:55. Hustle to your seats for our speaker" said Whitlock as she sprinted to open the auditorium doors.

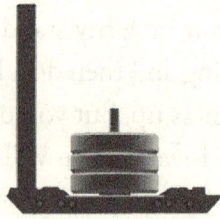

CHAPTER 62
PUT THE SHOPPING CART BACK

Our Winning Edge Wednesday speaker was an All-American softball player at Oklahoma State University, Josie Turley. Josie was a former Pine Lake star athlete and had a reputation as one of the most well-rounded and elite graduates our school had ever had.

"What up, Frogs? Great to see y'all," Josie said with a big smile. "Being here sure makes me miss my high school days.

"But hey, college is fun. I'll tell y'all, though, it was a serious adjustment for me. I got to campus and, wow, all my teammates were the best players from their high school. My first year, I only played in scrimmages.

"I started to doubt myself and often wondered if I would ever see the field in a real game. I was working hard on the field every day, but it wasn't quite enough. One of my biggest breakthroughs actually came off the field when I focused and became more aware of what I was putting in my body.

"In high school," Josie laughed, "I basically ate and drank whatever I wanted whenever I wanted. Before my sophomore year at OSU, we all met with Missy, the new college dietician. She talked with each of us about what type of foods we liked, didn't like, allergies, all that stuff. When Missy and I looked at my food journal for the week, I was kind of embarrassed. I had no idea how little protein I was getting in my system.

"She put together a specific food plan for each one of us and taught us a valuable lesson that **food is fuel**. I fought it at first. It takes time to break old habits and routines. But I wasn't seeing the field, so what the heck? I started small, and I couldn't believe the difference I started to see in my energy, performance, and recovery.

"That STEM thing Coach Whitlock taught y'all on Monday is for real. Listen to me saying 'y'all.' See, that's what living in Oklahoma does to a person," Josie joked.

"Anyway, when I started to see the advantage nutrition had on my performance, I decided to add a minor in sports nutrition to my business major. My goal after college is to start my own business as a sports nutritionist.

"To learn more about the food industry, I'm interning with Whole Foods this summer. Before any intern gets to go to corporate, we're required to spend the first two weeks working in the store. I tell y'all, I'm learning a lot about business, nutrition, and people this summer. If you get a chance to intern, take it. Even if you don't get paid, the experience is priceless.

"Okay, you heard enough about me. Let's talk about you. If any of y'all want some help on nutrition, DM me. I'm not an expert yet, but I can get you going in the right direction.

"Now, it sounds like you heard some great information on habits and routines on Monday. So, here's my question for you. When you go to a store and you use a shopping cart, do you put it back?

"This has become my pet peeve." Josie's tone turned from being a stand-up comedian to an agitated coach. "I bet about half of our shoppers just leave the cart in the parking lot for someone else to deal with. Then, people have to get out of their car, move the cart that's in a parking spot, then park. Talk about being arrogant.

"Frogs, don't be that person. Arrogance is ugly. People in this community know who you are, even if you don't know them. Let's send a message that Pine Lake athletes put the shopping carts back. That's it. It's very simple.

"It's a little thing that says everything about you, your character, your habits, and who you are at your core. Are you someone who is going to take a shortcut and leave a job undone? Or are you going to see it through to the finish? I mean, how will y'all win a championship if you don't even put the stinkin' shopping cart back?

"The shopping cart ain't heavy. It's not like the sleds y'all have been pushin' this summer. It's a matter of effort, habit, attention to detail, and doing the right thing. Even when no one is watching.

"Our hitting coach's favorite phase is, '**Excellence in small things leads to excellence in all things**.' Y'all know the shopping cart is just a symbol of what I'm talking about, right?"

We all nodded in agreement.

"If I could share one simple habit or routine that shows how little by little, a little becomes a lot, it would be to always have the mentality to the put the shopping cart back. By that I mean, put the shopping cart back in everything you do in school, sports, and life. You create that habit and routine, and I promise, you will see results in other areas like you've never seen before."

Josie pulled her glove from an OSU softball backpack. "See this right here?" she asked, pointing to the outside of her glove where the letters "PTSCB" were written in black marker.

"What's that stand for, Frogs?"

We all shouted, "Put the Shopping Cart Back!"

Josie made her point. It was clear and simple. It was easy to do but also easy not to do. Just last week, I had been at a grocery store with my mom, and I was too lazy to put the cart back. After hearing today's talk, that wouldn't happen again.

CHAPTER 63
MANAGING MENTAL ERRORS

After Josie's talk, Coach Whitlock explained the new sequence of five burpees, ten sit-ups, fifteen squats, and one set of Sled Jacks using the FROGS cadence. She also explained the twist of the integrity checks.

"A little incentive on this humid July day. As soon as the entire group can successfully complete a perfect series of the four exercises, you are done for the day," said Whitlock. This surprised the athletes who weren't at the 5:30 leadership training and brought a lot of smiles.

My boat crew got after it and started strong. We almost nailed it within the first five minutes, but a few athletes held themselves to the standard and owned their mistakes. It was tough to be mad at someone who took the "Put the Shopping Cart Back" message to heart.

The thought of getting done early must have been on most people's minds. Frustration grew as many athletes put extra pressure on themselves. Everyone knew a mistake would keep us from heading home early. We lost our focus and struggled with simply remembering what rep we were on. Twice, we were close to finishing the entire series, but a coach called up a mistake. One was called on Kinger. He not only made the mistake but didn't own up to it. This meant we now had to start over and add two reps to each exercise.

It took a lot longer than we all thought, which meant we didn't get to go home early. Nobody was happy about it. Coach Bobby read the frustration and brought us all to the fifty-yard line.

"There were a lot of lessons out there today," Bobby said. "To be real with you, I also saw some challenges in your focus, awareness, and personal integrity. It appeared that many of you focused on an outcome of getting done early, instead of the process of executing and doing it right.

"We put the 'end early' incentive out there as a bit of a test for you. Let's face it, being an athlete will test you, too. Hey, if a test is too easy, it won't challenge you. **If it doesn't challenge you, it won't change you.** You wouldn't be in sports if you didn't want to be tested and challenged.

"Almost all the mistakes were mental, not physical. Oftentimes, victories come down to which team or individual made the fewest number of mental errors." Bobby looked right at Kinger. "Right, Kinger?"

Kinger stared back at Bobby like an MMA fighter about to step into the octagon.

"Josie was on point this morning. If you are serious about the 'put the shopping cart back' mentality, my bet is you're going to win some games and competitions this year that you would have lost in the past. Today's experience, and really every experience you have in life, will create an opportunity to learn and improve," Bobby said in a direct tone we weren't used to hearing.

CHAPTER 64
WIN OR LOSE WE LEARN

"You know what you learn when you fall short of a gold medal by .026 of a second? When you miss your Olympic dream by that much?" Bobby asked as he held up his right thumb and index finger together.

"Whether we win or lose, the process is still the same. We need to search for lessons to learn and improve. Regardless of the outcome, we can choose to step forward into growth or back into safety. **We can either get bitter or get better.** The choice is yours. Let's debrief today's experience. Turn to somebody next to you and discuss what happened today."

I immediately looked to my left and met eyes with Kinger, and he was hot.

"This is BS, man. Calling me out like that. Making me look like an idiot in front of everyone. Screw these guys. I'm over the early mornings, dumb leadership activities, and don't get me started on pushing that frickin' sled. I'm the best athlete out here, and they don't even care!" Kinger said with a clenched fist and a tight jaw.

My initial response would have been to put him in his place and to address his lack of integrity, but instead I chose to listen and hear him out. He continued to bad-mouth the sled series, summer conditioning, Bobby, and Coach Whitlock. When he was finally done with his rant, I couldn't hold back anymore.

CHAPTER 65
ENOUGH IS ENOUGH

"So, it's the coaches' fault we weren't able to finish early?" I asked as if I couldn't believe he just said that.

Kinger's face turned as red as ketchup. "Jackson, you're such an A-hole." Kinger and I were about ten steps from the group when it started to heat up. As we went back and forth, our voices got louder, and we inched closer to each other. I felt myself about to lose my cool. The last thing I wanted to do was get into a fight with Kinger in front of everyone. Not exactly the look of a team captain. Plus, I knew that wouldn't end in my favor. But as an elected team captain, I also knew that my teammates expected me to lead them through the tough times. That meant I had to draw a line in the sand and stand up to the star of the team. I had had enough of his excuses and selfishness, and I was done putting up with his crap.

"You just don't get it, do you Kinger? You never have and probably never will. It's never your fault! You never take ownership. Like today, you clearly messed up and didn't own it. You pull everyone down like a drain. You think it's all about you. Plus, your stupid little comebacks aren't funny. People may laugh but not because it's funny. They laugh because the 'King of Comebacks' thinks he's funny. You wanna know why you weren't selected a team captain, Kinger? Well, mystery solved!"

My face was now as red as Kinger's, and I could feel my heart pounding. Even though I had been dreaming about saying all of this to him, I was surprised I actually did.

Suddenly, Kinger charged at me like a blitzing linebacker. My feet flew up in the air as he tackled me to the turf. It was one of the hardest hits I had ever taken.

Coach Bobby raced toward us before any punches were thrown, "Boys, boys, what's going on here?" he yelled as he separated us.

We both stood up and continued to glare at each other breathing heavy.

"I'll tell you what's going on. As my old man would say, 'Jackson's mouth is writing checks his body can't cash!'" Kinger said.

"Let's all take a deep breath and head to the end zone," Bobby said sternly.

My heart continued to pound out of my chest. I could barely breathe. Everyone stared at us as we walked by. I saw Olivia wipe a tear and turn away. I hadn't seen her cry since our parents got divorced. I was in shock at what just happened.

Bobby walked between Kinger and me. Once we were in the endzone, Bobby started the conversation the way he normally did. "David, what's on your mind?"

"Jackson told me I wasn't selected captain because I don't take ownership. I take ownership all day long. I also own about ten school records. Does that count for anything Bob O?" asked Kinger. I had never heard an athlete be so disrespectful to a coach in my life.

"David, there is no doubt you are a great football player and a great athlete. One of the best I've seen at your age."

I looked at Bobby. Nobody called Kinger by his first name.

"Yeah Bobby? Well, maybe tell that to this guy who choked and threw the interception in this very end zone," Kinger said as he angrily pointed at me.

"How talented you are between the lines is one thing. How you are as a person and as a leader in the classroom, weight room, or locker room is another thing," Bobby said. Are you opposed to me asking you some tough questions, David?"

"Nope. Isn't that what you're all about, asking better questions? The whole 'Get curious not furious garbage.' What questions ya got there, Bobsled Bobberino?" Kinger's tone was salty.

"Did you make your bed this morning?" asked Bobby, who was a calm as a late-night radio host.

"Nope," Kinger said.

"Have you made it at all this summer?" asked Bobby.

"Nope. Just a waste of time,"snapped back.

"Yesterday, I saw you at Whole Foods. Were you one of the people Josie talked about who didn't put the shopping cart back?"

"I didn't, but neither does half the population, according to her nonscientific study," Kinger said.

"Have you been filling out your success checklist on HabitShare?"

"Nope. I check stuff off in my head," Kinger replied.

He just doesn't get it. This conversation felt like it was going nowhere,
I thought.

CHAPTER 66
I HAD NO IDEA

"I have one more question, but I want you to really think about it before you answer." Bobby paused and his voice softened, "David... what do you think it's like being your teammate?"

"That's easy," Kinger blurted out immediately. "I'm an awesome teammate. The only All-Conference running back we got. Ran for over twelve hundred yards and eighteen touchdowns last year. And if the handoff would've been clean, I would have broken the single game record for touchdowns. What else do you want from me?"

"Those are your stats, David," said Bobby. "I'm asking, **what do you really think it's like to be your teammate?**"

Repeating the question appeared to catch Kinger off guard. He started to say something, then turned away for what felt like five minutes and didn't say anything. When he finally turned back to us, he looked like a different guy. His voice weakened and he stared at the ground.

"I don't know. Probably not a lot of fun, I guess. As much as I hate it, sometimes I catch myself acting and sounding just like my old man. The guy never has anything positive to say to me or anyone else. Probably why my mom left him seven years ago. Yeah, in fact, it's seven years ago today. I'll never forget that argument. Surprised the cops weren't called."

I had no idea Kinger's mom had been out of the picture for so long.

"The guy loves his alcohol. A drink is never far from his reach. He goes to happy hour at Wobbly Joe's with a bunch of other parents before every game. He gets all loaded up and then yells at me from the stands about what I'm doing wrong. You think I don't hear that? Why do parents have to drink before going to a high school game? I hate it. The drinking continues after the game, too. You should see it. He usually has another six-pack down by the time I get home. I can't even put my bag down before I get the ESPN play-by-play of everything I could have done better. It's never good enough for him.

"Action, remember last year against Tri-Valley when I scored five touchdowns?" asked Kinger.

"Yeah, that was your best game," I said.

"You know what he said when I got home? 'Nice try, kid. Still not quite as good as me. Looks like the single game touchdown record at Pine Lake still has my name on it. What can I say? When you're good, you're good.'" Kinger's eyes started to water.

A single tear fell as Kinger continued, "Then he points to himself and said, 'Hey, how about number one and number two go to Wobbly Joe's for pizza and celebrate that the school record is still in the right person's hands? Could have been yours if not for the fumble in the second quarter, Butterfingers.'

"Here's the real sad part. I went with him. Can you believe that? I went with him! I had to drive because he was too loaded." Kinger was a mess, and the tears were streaming.

I also started to get emotional. I couldn't believe it. I had no idea what Kinger was dealing with at home. On this day, seven years ago, his mom left. No wonder he was all wound up today. It explained a lot about him.

CHAPTER 67
THE BREAKTHROUGH

After a minute of silence, Bobby gently continued, "I'm sorry to hear that. Thank you for being vulnerable and real. Difficult, no doubt."

He went on, "Look, David, the only thing Coach Whitlock, Coach Allen, Jackson, and I want from you is for you to become the best version of yourself. That's why we called you up for an integrity check during the sled series today."

"Believe it or not, even though I have all those school records, sometimes I feel like I'm a total screw up," said Kinger.

Bobby responded, "Making new mistakes and owning them is making progress in disguise. However, part of the process is being able to manage your emotions and sift through the embarrassment, tears, struggles, and adversities so you can pull those lessons out for the future.

"How about looking at a failure as an event and not as an identifying factor of who you are as a person?" Bobby asked.

"David, we all see what you can be. Average athletes want to be left alone. Good athletes want to be coached. Great athletes want the truth. What do you want?"

"I want to be great. Not sure I can handle it though. We've come this far, what's the truth?" Kinger asked like he really wanted to know.

"The truth is you have the potential to be the best football player ever to play at Pine Lake. More importantly, you also have the potential to be an amazing leader and teammate. You weren't elected a team captain, but you don't have to be a team captain to be a team leader.

"We can either learn from the past or live in the past. David, your past doesn't have to become your future. Yes, you have a lot of junk to deal with at home. Nobody knows what that's like for you. It's good that you're aware you can fall into the trap of sounding like your dad. But it sounds like you don't want to be that guy anymore."

Kinger shook his head and said, "No way. That's not who I want to be. But it's hard when that's all you know."

"Hey, Kinger, I'm sorry, man. I didn't know you were dealing with all that stuff," was all I could say.

"It's okay, Action, no one knows. That's why I never have anyone at my house. Even if he's not drinking, I never know when the old man is gonna go off," Kinger said.

Bobby jumped in, "As rough as today was, breakdowns can lead to breakthroughs. Maybe today is the day you start to take your preparation, your leadership, and yourself more seriously."

Kinger nodded slowly. "Maybe. Just seems like I got a long way to go," he said humbly as he shook his head.

Bobby picked up the pieces as only a seasoned coach could and asked, "How do you want to move forward from here?"

Kinger took a deep breath and let out a long exhale. "First, I owe you both an apology. Can't believe I went after Jackson like that in front of everyone. I'm sorry for acting like an idiot today and being a jerk this whole summer.

"Second, it's time to start being a better teammate and a better leader. That question you asked me about what's it like being my teammate really made me think. I'm going to start doing this stuff you've been talking about. Make my bed, put the shopping cart back, stay curious. All of it. I'm going to start being a fountain instead of a drain and stop making excuses when I screw up. I want to make the most of my last year in high school. Who knows if I will play in college anyway?"

"Thanks, Bobby. Thanks for caring and calling me up. You too, Action," Kinger said as he wiped the tears from his eyes. "I will get better."

"I think you just did," Coach Bobby said.

"Action, can you get with Kinger this weekend and help him dial in his success checklist on HabitShare?"

I knew we were in a better spot when Bobby started calling him Kinger.

"Happy to, Coach. I got you, Kinger," I said and pointed at him.

"Kinger, if Action is going to take the time to help you create your success checklist, review the Tactical Skills, and go through all the drills, will you commit to doing the work?"

"Yes sir. I will," Kinger said.

After a bro hug, Kinger and I walked to the parking lot together. We were both surprised to see Olivia and Faith talking by their cars. They were surprised to see us too.

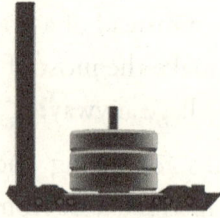

CHAPTER 68
A MEETING OF THE MINDS

"What in the world was that about!?" asked Oliva, who was still emotional. Faith looked shook up too.

Kinger and I looked at each other, not knowing exactly what to say.

"There was a lot of stuff we both had on our minds, and guess it finally came out," I said.

"No kidding. But a fight in front of everyone? I mean, come on. That's not right at all," said Faith.

"You're right," Kinger said humbly. "I'll take the blame on that one. Jackson called me out, I mean called me up, and I didn't take it very well. I let emotions get the best of me, and I lost it for a second. It's on me."

"To be fair, part of the blame goes to me," I said. "There were a lot of things I thought I knew about Kinger. Turns out, I didn't know much at all."

"We're sorry," Kinger and I both said together. The timing made both of us laugh. Even though we had a long way to go, for the first time ever, it felt like we could actually become friends... someday.

"Bobby helped us sort it all out. We still have some stuff to talk about, but I think we will be able to work through it. We both know it was the wrong place and the wrong time. The good thing is we're in a much better spot now."

Kinger jumped in, "Can you two forgive a couple of fools who lost their cool for few minutes? We're sorry, and we promise it won't happen again."

The girls looked at each other and hesitated. Finally, Faith said, "I guess I can. What about you, Olivia?"

"Well, I'm used to my brother being a fool, so it's just another chapter for me. So yeah, I'm sure I'll tuck this one away and bring it up in the future when I need to embarrass him like he embarrassed me with that fight," she said with a comedic smirk.

"Okay, I'm going to pull a Dax line here," said Faith as she smiled. 'Seems Olivia and I are in a bit of a *pickle,* and we need you two clowns to help us out of it."

"Name it," Kinger said.

CHAPTER 69
DOUBLES, ANYONE?

"Olivia's doubles partner twisted her ankle yesterday. They registered for the community wide pickleball tournament this weekend. No way her partner can play. So, instead of withdrawing, Olivia asked me to join her." Faith's expression looked just like Dax's when he delivered a one liner during the second Winning Edge Wednesday on Focus and Awareness.

"Here's the *pickle* we are in," laughed Faith out loud. "Olivia and I haven't played together as doubles partners. And we don't plan to participate, we plan to dominate. We want to play you two tonight and see how we do."

That was all Kinger and I needed to hear. "Game on," said Kinger.

"What are we playing for?" I asked.

"Losers wash the winners' cars," said Faith.

"Better bring your soap and buckets, because my car is filthy," said Kinger. While his words didn't surprise me, his tone was much more positive.

Olivia asked, "How about dinner at our place first?"

"Sounds good. I always like being at your house," said Kinger.

Instead of rolling my eyes, I smiled. If I had to deal with Kinger's home life, I would enjoy being at my house too.

After Kinger and I did the Champions Do More workout that afternoon, we went to Whole Foods to get everything we needed to make spaghetti. Kinger insisted that he would put the shopping cart back. His new approach was refreshing, I just wondered if it would last.

Even though I burned the breadsticks, dinner was a blast. It was the first time we were all in the same room with no drama or negative vibes.

We went to the pickleball court and played until dark, Kinger and I did all we could to keep up with Liv and Faith. While the prize was to get our cars washed, it was more about each team wanting to show the other they were better. That's what you get when four competitive athletes who hate to lose go head-to-head.

After the friendly, or not-so-friendly, competition, Kinger and I said we would wash their cars after the tournament on Sunday.

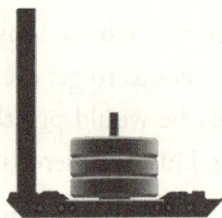

CHAPTER 70
WE ARE THE CHAMPIONS

The pickleball tournament went on all weekend.

Kinger and I watched the girls play on Saturday, but Sunday we met at the field to go through our handoffs, pitches, and screen passes. Kinger even volunteered to run long routes so I could work on my footwork and timing. We talked about how we could use the Tactical Skills in the upcoming season. We also dove into completing the drills Kinger blew off.

When we arrived home, Queen's "We Are the Champions" was pumping through the house and there was a huge trophy on our kitchen table.

"You won?" I asked Liv.

"We didn't just win, we dominated! Faith can play," said Olivia. "That girl is a baller, and believe it or not, we used some of the stuff we learned this summer."

"Like what?" I asked.

"Stuff from Coach Buzz. It started with a contingency plan. Somebody stepped on my paddle and broke it. Thankfully, Faith had thrown an extra one in her bag," said Olivia.

"And I was so nervous before the championship match," said Faith. "Then Olivia reminded me what Coach Buzz said. That I could be confident and nervous at the same time and that pressure is a privilege."

I couldn't believe it. What had happened to my sister? She was a different human.

Both girls giggled when they handed Kinger and I buckets, sponges, and soap.

Kinger, the King of Comebacks, didn't have a clever one ready. All he could say was, "We want a rematch."

"Anytime," the girls said in sync.

So, we took the supplies and headed to the driveway to live up to our end of the deal.

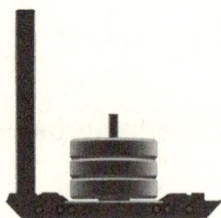

CHAPTER 71
TACTICAL SKILL #7 – UNSHAKABLE SELF-CONFIDENCE

"CHECK IN!" Coach Whitlock said.

"ALL IN!" we echoed back.

"You've made it to our last Mental Performance Monday. Let's celebrate that!" Coach Whitlock said as everyone applauded.

"Tactical Skill #7 is Unshakable Self-Confidence. We could spend hours debating questions like the ones on the screen."

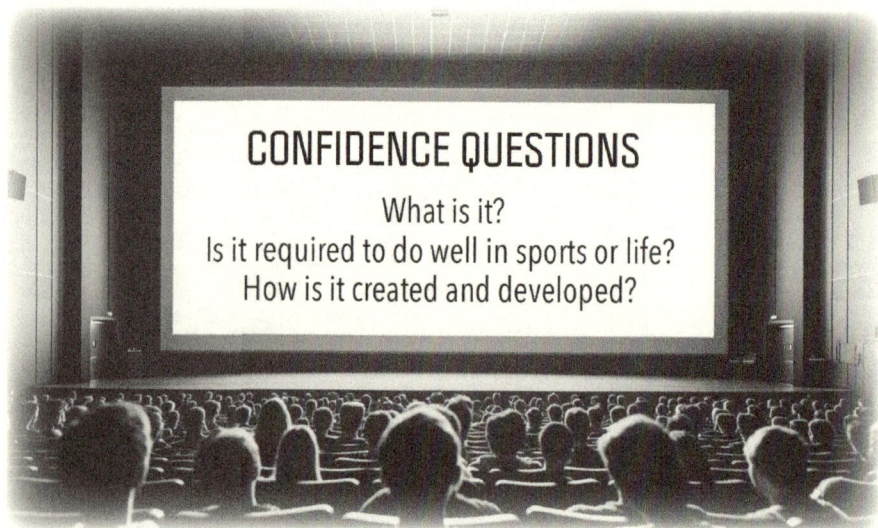

CONFIDENCE QUESTIONS
What is it?
Is it required to do well in sports or life?
How is it created and developed?

"Let's start with the first one. What is confidence? I think Dr. Nate Zinsser, author of *The Confident Mind*, said it best."

Coach Whitlock used a laser beam to point at a quote on the screen.

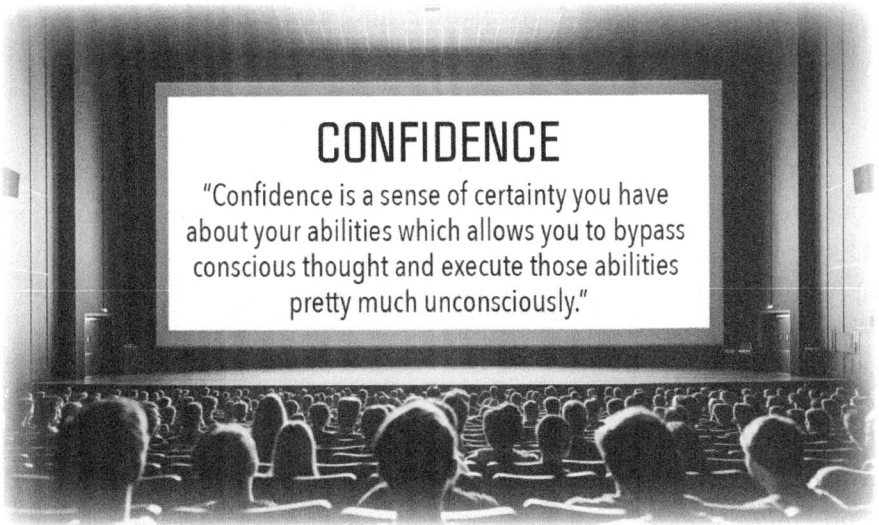

CONFIDENCE

"Confidence is a sense of certainty you have about your abilities which allows you to bypass conscious thought and execute those abilities pretty much unconsciously."

In other words, confidence is about believing and trusting in your capabilities. Fun fact, the words confidence actually comes from two latin words *con+fidere* which means intense inner trust.

"On an episode from The Mindset Advantage podcast, Dr. Z used the example of how we walk up a flight of stairs. 'You aren't thinking about what muscles to use, where your feet need to land, or where your eyes should look as you climb the stairs. These thoughts aren't necessary because you have had so many reps doing it that it's now automatic.'

"Okay, question number two," continued Whitlock, "Is confidence required to do well in sports or life? Coach Buzz talked about this two weeks ago.

"How many of you have walked into an exam not feeling very confident, but still ended up with a good score?" Whitlock asked.

Almost everyone raised their hand.

"How many of you have walked into an exam feeling very confident and ended up with a lousy grade?"

Even more hands went in the air.

"Based on how you responded, it's clear that you don't *have* to have confidence to be successful. However, I think we would all agree, it's more advantageous to feel confident than not.

"Finally, how is confidence created and developed?

"I like to compare confidence to a windmill. The main tower represents your preparation. That's why this summer program was named Separation Through Preparation. We've been preparing all summer so you can be physically capable and mentally unshakable before the year starts.

"The drills like MVP, Well–Better–How, Concentration Grids, Shadow Work, and, Power Phrases are all designed to build a better you. **Average athletes hate the drills yet want the skills.** Those of you who did the drills also acquired new skills and as a byproduct have gained more confidence.

CHAPTER 72
BFS

"So, the tower of a windmill represents how preparation can build confidence *before* a competition. But how can you build confidence during competition when the pressure is on? For example, when you go into extra innings, overtime, sudden death, whatever it is in your sport, it can feel like all eyes are on you. How can you have Unshakable Self-Confidence during one of those nail-biting, real time moments when it gets 'icy and dicey' as we used to say in bobsledding?" Whitlock asked rhetorically as she flipped to the next slide.

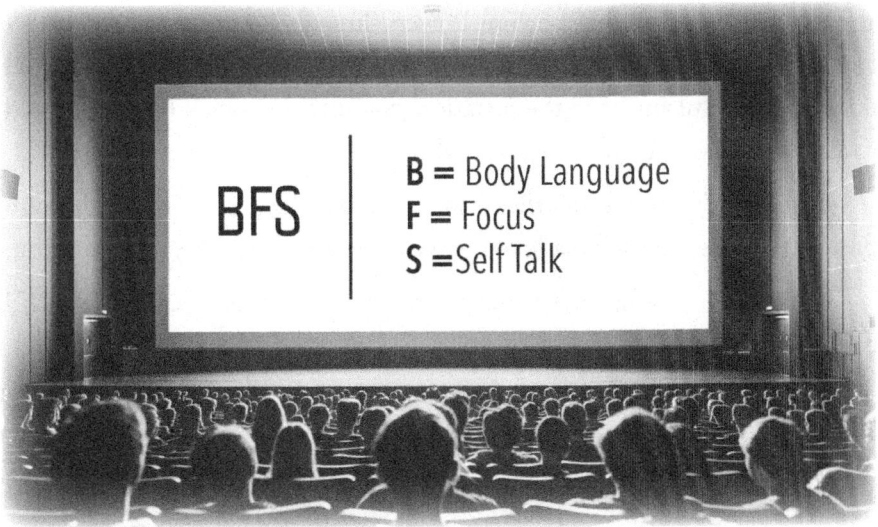

BFS	B = Body Language
	F = Focus
	S = Self Talk

"You create confidence *during* competition by being aware of each blade of the windmill. BFS."

Your *body language* needs to be big, tall, and unstoppable. Recent research says it's best to have your feet shoulder width apart when possible. Put your weight on the center of your feet. Let's not sway or rock back and forth or side to side as it can send a bad message to your brain that you are tentative or unsure. This not only will help you but it also sends a message to your teammates and your opponent.

During Olympic training we watched a Ted Talk by social psychologist, Amy Cuddy. She said, **"Your mind affects your body, and your body affects your mind. In addition, our bodies change our minds. Our minds change our behavior. Our behavior changes our outcome.**

Your *focus* needs to stay in the present moment while you prepare and while you compete. In either case, think about what you need to do now. It's easy to start to get ahead of yourself. Focus on what you can control. Avoid getting sucked into the outside distractions or paying unnecessary attention to the other team or the crowd.

Finally, *self-talk*. You've heard this a lot this summer. You want to talk to yourself instead of listening to yourself. Fill your mind up with positive and productive self-talk. Use your Power Phrase, use the word YET, don't complain, ask yourself better questions, avoid absolutes like always and never, be grateful you're in the situation, encourage yourself like you would if you were talking to your best friend.

Today, let's appreciate the personal tower you have built through preparation and get each blade of the windmill moving to create separation.

"How about we harness some personal electricity and have a powerful day? Let's get some!"

We all clapped with enthusiasm.

With that, we closed our training manuals and headed outside to see what Coach Bobby had in store for us.

CHAPTER 73
UNFINISHED BUSINESS

Our last Winning Edge Wednesday of the summer featured our school's social media director, Andrea Armstrong. In her short time at PLHS, she had been able to live stream all our games, record our practices, make banners and posters, and create highlight films for all activities.

Armstrong took the stage wearing a high-tech headset mic. "You all have seen me and some volunteers with cameras and drones filming this summer. You probably wondered what we were doing."

The auditorium went dark. The music slowly picked up. The video started with the kickoff meeting on the last day of school where Coach Allen introduced us to Coach Whitlock and Coach Bobby.

All the coaches, athletes, and speakers were featured. *I can't believe she was able to capture all of this,* I thought.

The video showed all the tactical skills and drills, the 5:30 leadership sessions and, of course, the sled workouts. She even caught the moment when I was exhausted and wanted to stop pushing the sled.

Everyone, including me, laughed when they saw my red face fill the screen.

At the end were the words...

UNFINISED BUSINESS.

CHAPTER 74
DRILL #12 - PERSONAL HIGHLIGHT REEL

"I'll tell you, Frogs, I got a kick out of putting that video together," Armstrong said. You've probably heard the phrase 'A picture is worth a thousand words.' If that's true, imagine how much a video is worth?

"I've been following along and learning this summer, too. And after hearing Coach Whitlock talk about unshakable confidence on Monday, I had to ask her if I could share my favorite drill with you."

"A lot of us spend hours scrolling through other people's highlight reels on social. I believe we can use our profiles for more than just 'likes.' Plus, the vast majority of people are visual learners, so let's use that to our advantage.

"Drill #12 is to build a personal highlight reel.

"One of the many ways to gain Unshakable Self-Confidence is to have a way to see yourself performing at your best. Here's what you do. Collect a combination of pictures and videos that are meaningful and motivating to you. These could be pictures with friends and family or videos from your best performances. You could even create a reel of your favorite college or professional athlete performing in your sport. Then put those in a folder on your phone, or you could get fancy and make a highlight reel. You could also do a vision screen by adding a collection of photos or screen shots as the background on your phone. Every time you go to your phone, you're sending a positive message to your brain.

"The best time to look at the photos or watch the video is the moment before you step out to the court, field, or platform. **You must see it to be it.**

"If you start walking around with big body language, focusing on the present moment and what you can control, and talk to yourself instead of listen to yourself, self-confidence is going to ooze out of you like mayonnaise on a sandwich!"

The personal highlight drill made perfect sense to me. I loved watching highlights on ESPN. As Armstrong started to wrap up, I thought about what pictures and plays would be on my reel. I'm going to keep the 14-13 on my phone as motivation to prove others wrong. But, I need to add more images to my vision screen to prove myself right. Adding a highlight reel and a vision screen to my phone is going to be a game changer for me.

We gave Armstrong an enthusiastic round of applause, closed our notebooks, and headed out to the fields for a Sled Jack warm-up followed by another sled workout that would test us all.

CHAPTER 75
FINISH STRONG

After the workout, Bobby had us take a knee.

"Frogs, even though we fell short of our standard a few times, it was still a good day," Bobby said. "**When we meet the standards, the outcome will take care of itself.**"

"You trained with focus and awareness, self-control, and discipline. You got curious instead of furious. You stayed in your routine and worked the process. Despite a few setbacks, your body language was big, tall, and unstoppable. We're not done yet. As you saw in the amazing video Ms. Armstrong put together, we still have some unfinished business. Tomorrow we will be back on the sleds in the stadium for one more grinder of a workout.

"Back in my bobsled days, my favorite part was when we came around the final stretch of the track at ninety miles per hour. No way the brake would be touched at that point. We were nervous and excited at the same time. All the crazy turns were behind us, and it was just us going all out to the finish line. Talking about it still gives me goosebumps, even though it's ninety degrees. That's where you are right now. Let's not stop until we get across the finish line.

"Alright, bring it in for a breakdown."

"One... two... three... Finish Strong!" we all yelled.

CHAPTER 76
THE FINAL DAY

It was hard to believe the last day had arrived. I was not the same person I was at the beginning of camp. I was bigger, stronger, faster, and more agile than ever. My mental game still needed work, but it was clearly better. And I knew if I used the drills and skills Coach Whitlock and Bobby provided, I could continue to improve. It was cool to see that many of the early doubters and bashers of the program, started to buy into the new system. This was going to be a year to remember.

We entered the auditorium and saw a list of names on the screen.

"If you see your name up here today, please come to the stage," said Coach Whitlock. "Coach Allen has a special shirt for you." Music blasted and colored lights were spinning throughout the auditorium. It felt like the introductions at a Minnesota Timberwolves or Lynx game.

Olivia, Faith, Kinger and I, along with at least forty others, received a sweet UNRL brand shirt.

"These shirts are symbolic of having to adapt your summer plans to attend all twenty-eight training sessions. **Nothing of value can be given, it must be earned.** You earned these shirts through your commitment and dedication to training.

"Let's celebrate these athletes and their commitment to a new process with a round of applause," Coach Whitlock said.

"We started with a hundred fifty athletes in June. To have one hundred thirty show up for the final workout is impressive.

Coach Allen interjected, "That's never happened, and it says a lot about EVERYONE in this auditorium."

Coach Whitlock smiled and nodded at Coach Allen and continued, "Each of you are a part of a new era. No longer is 'good enough' our standard. We are no longer here to participate. We are here to dominate. From now on, the competition is *playing you*. You are not *playing them*. We are the Ferocious Frogs of Pine Lake!"

Coach Whitlock was getting fired up in a way that only a passionate coach who truly cared about students could.

Everyone started to clap and cheer.

"We have unfinished business. Today we have a finale series of sled jacks to complete. But we will no longer spell out F-R-O-G-S, instead we will spell out F-I-N-I-S-H."

"Let's go to work!"

With that, we all headed out to the stadium, where we saw freshly painted lines and our school's Frog mascot painted in the end zones.

The field was game-ready and so were we.

CHAPTER 77
EXECUTION

Each Winning Edge Wednesday speaker was there to watch our last workout. The only exception was Matt Carpenter, who joined us via FaceTime.

Coach Bobby called on Olivia to lead the F-I-N-I-S-H sequence. The new cadence threw us off at first, but we adapted.

Athletes called themselves on mistakes during integrity checks the first two attempts. Rep three was perfect. I was proud of my sister, who didn't hesitate to lead the first round when her name was called. She actually seemed to enjoy the role of being in front of the group.

Bobby called on Faith to be our second large group leader. Suddenly, Coach Whitlock turned on some pump-up music from the press box. We didn't know if this was to fire us up or to distract us. The music didn't faze Faith. To no one's surprise, she led the group to a perfect set of evolutions on the second attempt.

Whitlock replaced the music with a soundtrack of a large crowd. It sounded like we were playing in a huge stadium at a major college. I didn't expect it, but I kind of liked the extra challenge of hearing the crowd noise and overcoming it. If I hadn't personally messed up, we would have nailed it on the first try.

"Action!" yelled Coach Bobby over the fake crowd noise, you're up!"

I sprinted to the front of the group and stood next to Bobby.

"You're a team captain. You have been here for every workout this summer. You've done everything we've asked you to do, from pushing the sled to attending every 5:30 leadership session. Plus, the work you did for the Champions Do More workouts didn't go unnoticed.

We have one evolution of sled jacks left, and it's got a major twist. You're going to take us home. You ready?

"Coach, with all due respect I'd like to finish this with somebody by my side," Bobby held up both hands, and Whitlock paused the soundtrack.

"I'd like to give Kinger the opportunity to join me. He's the best player on our team, the best athlete in our school, and if we're going to have a season of significance, we will need him to play a major role and lead us in the right direction."

I said all this as I looked directly at him. Our eyes were glued. He looked surprised and emotional. So did the other 138 athletes who stuck with the Separation Through Preparation program.

Coach Bobby hammered his whistle one more time. "Kinger, join Action up front!" he shouted.

Everyone clapped and yelled for him. We gave each other a loud high five as we stood next to each other.

Together we yelled, "CHECK IN!"

"ALL IN!" everyone shouted in unison. It was badass.

"Everyone, take deep breath. Focus on what we're doing. Ignore the noise and be where your feet are!" yelled Kinger.

Just as we were about to start, the major twist was unveiled. All the coaches pulled out a combination of air horns, cowbells, and other noisemakers. Whitlock also cranked the crowd noise to the max. It was by far the loudest this stadium had ever been.

Kinger smiled at me, gave me nod, and said, "Game on!"

I could feel the intensity and focus from all one hundred thirty-eight athletes. We were ready to finish what we started two months ago. Despite all the distractions, there were no integrity violations.

We did it! We finished the Separation Through Preparation summer training. We all ran to the center of the field and jumped up and down, celebrating our success around Coach Bobby and Coach Whitlock.

I had yet to win a State Championship at Pine Lake, but I had to imagine that's what the feeling would be like. It was incredible.

CHAPTER 78
PUSH THE SLED

Coach Whitlock blew her whistle and had everyone take a knee.

"Kinger, that was amazing. That's the type of comeback statement we are looking for you to make this year! Nice work. What did you think when Jackson called you up to join him for the final evolution of the summer?" Whitlock asked.

"I wasn't expecting to get called up like that. I'm not gonna lie, I was nervous," Kinger said. "But I just acted different than how I felt, and you know what? It worked."

"It works when you work it. That's the lesson for every skill and drill we covered this summer," Coach Whitlock said.

I raised my hand. "Coach, can I say something?"

"Of course. What's on your mind?" asked Whitlock.

I stood up and made my way to the front of the crowd. "Coaches, you said this is the start of a new era, and we are excited about the new muscles and mindset you helped us build. We all feel a lot different physically and mentally than we did at the beginning of the summer. To show you our appreciation for all your hard work, Coach Bobby, and all the other coaches, we have a little surprise."

I signaled to Kinger, Olivia, and Faith to join me. They carried four rolled up green banners.

Olivia unrolled a banner with the words, Separation Through Preparation.

Faith's banner was Little by Little, a Little Becomes a Lot.

Kinger's banner was Push the Sled.

My banner was the biggest, standing as tall as I was. I asked a couple athletes to hold the ends for me. It listed each of the 7 Tactical Skills of an Elevated Mindset.

"Armstrong helped us design them and Coach Allen already knows where they will be hung up in the school," I said.

Whitlock paused and scanned the entire group of athletes. Her eyes welled up. Finally, with a shaky voice, she said, "Those are amazing! What a summer. Thank you all for making my first summer ever at Pine Lake a memorable one. Thank you to all the coaches who showed up every day and brought the juice. Thanks to all the speakers who took time out of their busy schedule to make a transformational impact. The watery eyes turned to a few tears. "Finally, thanks to my dad for his expertise on the mental game and on the sleds. Doing this as a father-daughter team is something I'll always cherish."

Coach Bobby stepped in and looked his daughter in the eyes. "Jess, I enjoyed every minute of this experiment and experience."

He then turned to the group and said, "**It's not about being temporary. It's about being legendary.**"

"That's what separation through preparation and pushing the sled is all about. Frogs, that's the new standard. Don't count the days, make the days count. Let's make each day of this new year count. Two claps if you're with me," Coach Bobby said.

Everyone loudly clapped their hands twice.

"Oh, one last thing," said Whitlock. "I have a surprise for you. Bobsled Bobby planned to head south after my renovation was complete. Well, he enjoyed working with the Ferocious Frogs of Pine Lake so much, he bought a fixer upper of his own and is planning to stay for at least a year.

"Coach Allen heard the exciting news and invited him to conduct a new series of monthly leadership workshops for any student who is interested."

The applause was electric, which clearly impacted Bobby. She added, "This whole thing is a process, not an event. I believe we are just getting started. But for now, you've officially completed the Separation Through Preparation summer program.

Bobby and Coach Whitlock locked eyes, "Except, champions always do more."

"Sled pushes, anyone?" asked Bobby and Whitlock in unison with a joyful smile.

SEPARATION THROUGH PREPARATION

LITTLE BY LITTLE A LITTLE BECOMES A LOT

PUSH THE SLED

7 TACTICAL SKILLS

DEEP CURIOSITY

FOCUS & AWARENESS

PROCESS OVER OUTCOME

SELF-CONTROL AND
DISCIPLINE

VISUALIZATION

ROUTINES & HABITS OF
EXCELLENCE

UNSHAKABLE
SELF-CONFIDENCE

ABOUT THE AUTHORS

Craig Hillier started his speaking career as a college student. Since 1990, he has spoken to over two million people throughout the United States.

His keynotes and leadership workshops are known to be upbeat, fun, and educational.

The author of four books, Craig's <u>High School Sports Leader</u> book is used throughout the country as curriculum to develop team leaders and captains. www.highschoolsportsleader.com

Craig and Kelly were married in 1989 and enjoy living a few minutes away from their adult children DJ and Abigayle. They are over the top excited about becoming new grandparents. Just ask them!

To contact Craig about a speaking event:

craig@craighillier.com | www.craighillier.com

DJ Hillier has been transforming lives inside and outside of the fitness space for over a decade. He has competed at four regional CrossFit Competitions and one CrossFit Games alongside the top .01% of the fittest athletes in the world.

DJ is the host of The Mindset Advantage Podcast, where he interviews leading experts in the fields of Leadership, Mindset, and Fitness. DJ takes his personal experience along with the wisdom from his podcast guests to groups nationwide. His high energy keynotes and hands-on workshops focus on training athletes to use their mind to their advantage.

DJ's mission is to serve others and help people at every level attack the gap from where they are to where they want to be.

To contact DJ about coaching, consulting, or speaking:

dj@djhillier.com | www.djhillier.com

EXTRA PUSH SECTION

RESOURCES

To learn about using <u>Push the Sled</u> for a team and special package offers go to **www.pushthesled.com**

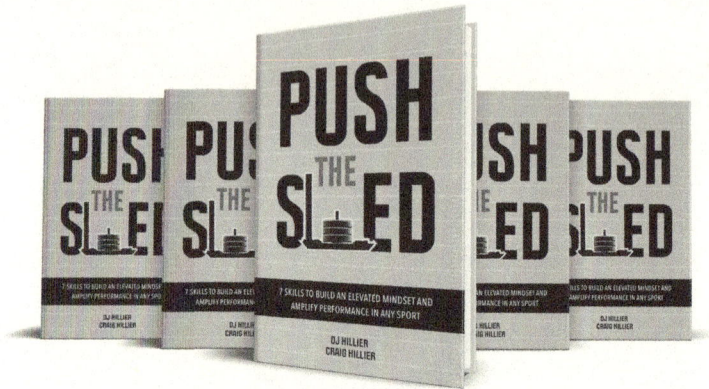

To listen to DJ Hillier's podcast, search **The Mindset Advantage** where ever you listen to podcasts. To watch the podcasts, go to YouTube and search for DJ Hillier.

To learn about Craig Hillier's book **High School Sports Leader** book go to:
www.highschoolsportsleader.com

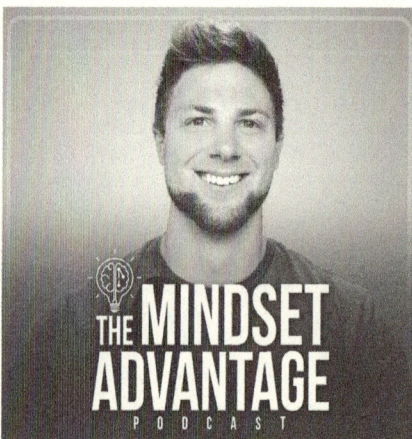

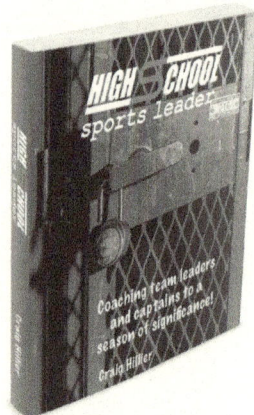

M.V.P. PROCESS

MISSION

I will be remembered as a
teammate who:

VISION

My vision is to:

PRINCIPLES

The principles that will guide my mission and vision are:

SUCCESS

Definition of Success for the Upcoming Season/Year:

ONE WORD INTENTION:

START - STOP - CONTINUE

START
What Do I Need to Start Doing Better?

STOP
What Do I Need to Stop Doing?

CONTINUE
What Do I Need to Continue Doing?

3 STEP RELEASE ROUTINE

POWER
THROUGH
PHRASE

DEEP
BREATH ON
A FOCAL
POINT

PHYSICAL
ACTION

MY 3-STEP RELEASE ROUTINE

1. PHYSICAL ACTION

2. DEEP BREATH ON A FOCAL POINT

3. POWER THROUGH PHRASE

CONCENTRATION GRID

39	05	10	16	14	48	19
28	24	17	21	45	44	43
07	04	23	18	12	13	29
46	15	02	31	36	00	37
01	03	47	30	08	41	20
40	11	42	06	33	25	26
35	34	38	22	27	09	32

TIME: _____

CONCENTRATION GRID

15	35	76	26	68	11	48	17	54	01
34	19	61	59	32	56	18	23	24	16
55	79	92	14	08	72	88	66	20	81
41	57	86	39	64	00	98	49	74	06
60	36	82	53	51	07	58	04	95	90
83	31	46	71	63	27	62	29	05	40
99	93	89	10	78	50	38	37	75	70
30	21	25	97	73	02	13	42	45	87
12	77	22	96	69	67	65	85	43	09
80	44	47	03	94	52	84	28	91	33

TIME: _____

WORKSHOP NOTES

WORKSHOP NOTES

WORKSHOP NOTES

WORKSHOP NOTES

Made in the USA
Middletown, DE
27 July 2024